Praise for *Call Down Lightning*

"A refreshment and challenge to my soul."

—Donald Mitchell, Union Theological Seminary, Byntirion, Bridgend, Wales

"God is ready to lift our society—all the ingredients are here: the lightning rods of God's people crying out in prayer are sparking a transformative, sustained movement of His relentless love. I heartily recommend a thorough reading of this insightful work. The formative clouds of revival cover our land; the wind of God is brooding over us, breeding life into our nation. 'The Lord reigns, let the earth rejoice . . . His lightnings light up the world; the earth sees and trembles' (Psalm 97:1–4 ESV)."

—Tom Phillips, vice president, Billy Graham Evangelistic Association; author of *Jesus Now Awakening*

"Words are inadequate to describe just how invigorating, thought-provoking, and motivating it was to read *Call Down Lightning*! Wallace Henley's unique gift of communicating stirs the heart and soul to learn from the lessons of revival and to re-dig from those wells with a hunger for a modern-day outpouring of the Holy Spirit. . . . I believe this book can be a catalyst to fan the flames for revival again. . . . Wallace Henley rightfully reminds us, 'In true revival, Jesus Christ is seen more clearly than ever.'"

—Doug Stringer, founder and president, Somebody Cares International; author of *Leadership Awakening*

CALL DOWN LIGHTNING

What the Welsh Revival of 1904
Reveals About the End Times

WALLACE HENLEY

EMANATE
BOOKS

Published in Nashville, Tennessee, by Emanate Books, an imprint of Thomas Nelson. Emanate Books and Thomas Nelson are registered trademarks of HarperCollins Christian Publishing, Inc.

Thomas Nelson titles may be purchased in bulk for educational, business, fund-raising, or sales promotional use. For information, please e-mail SpecialMarkets@ThomasNelson.com.

Unless otherwise noted, Scripture quotations are taken from New American Standard Bible®. Copyright © 1960, 1962, 1963, 1968, 1971, 1972, 1973, 1975, 1977, 1995 by The Lockman Foundation. Used by permission. (www.Lockman.org)

Scripture quotations marked KJV are from the King James Version. Public domain.

Scripture quotations marked NIV are from the Holy Bible, New International Version®, NIV®. Copyright © 1973, 1978, 1984, 2011 by Biblica, Inc.® Used by permission of Zondervan. All rights reserved worldwide. www.Zondervan.com. The "NIV" and "New International Version" are trademarks registered in the United States Patent and Trademark Office by Biblica, Inc.®

Scripture quotations marked NLT are from the Holy Bible, New Living Translation. © 1996, 2004, 2007, 2013, 2015 by Tyndale House Foundation. Used by permission of Tyndale House Publishers, Inc., Carol Stream, Illinois 60188. All rights reserved.

Any Internet addresses, phone numbers, or company or product information printed in this book are offered as a resource and are not intended in any way to be or to imply an endorsement by Thomas Nelson, nor does Thomas Nelson vouch for the existence, content, or services of these sites, phone numbers, companies, or products beyond the life of this book.

ISBN 978-0-7852-1911-8 (eBook)
ISBN 978-0-7852-1907-1 (TP)

Library of Congress Control Number: 2018961264

Printed in the United States of America
19 20 21 22 23 LSC 10 9 8 7 6 5 4 3 2 1

To the memory of
Dr. Billy Graham
Who went to heaven as this book was being finished

And to our great-grandchildren,
Victoria and Sofia Trejo, Jack Hesley,
and those yet to be born
May you see Jubilee in your lifetime

Contents

In the last days, God says,
I will pour out my Spirit on all people.
Your sons and daughters will prophesy,
your young men will see visions,
your old men will dream dreams.
Even on my servants, both men and women,
I will pour out my Spirit in those days,
and they will prophesy.
I will show wonders in the heavens above
and signs on the earth below.

—ACTS 2:17–19 NIV

Prologue

The *Gathering Storm* was the title Winston Churchill gave to the first volume of his history of the Second World War. In many ways that conflict, which ultimately became global, is a parable in human time of the war in the heavens (Rev. 12:7), the great battle for the advance of the kingdom of God in a world occupied by the powers of darkness (1 John 5:19).

Several years ago I coauthored *God and Churchill* with Jonathan Sandys, Churchill's great-grandson. After a year of probing Churchill's mind through his great-grandson's memories, I gained a small sense of what Churchill might have felt in 1939–40 as the storm of Adolf Hitler's blitz swept down on England.

Jonathan arranged for us to premiere the British version of the book at the Churchill War Rooms, the labyrinth beneath the streets of Whitehall, the London center of the British government. I had been in the War Rooms before, among tourists, but this time was special. I arrived early for the book premiere, and my wife, Irene, and I strolled through the War Rooms alone, sensing the weight and somber atmosphere of the place.

As a sixteen-year-old boy, Churchill had told a schoolmate that someday London would be under attack and that he would be in a high position and would save England and the British Empire. In 1939–40, when Britain stood alone against Hitler, Prime Minister Churchill might have forgotten the amazing prediction he had made decades earlier.

On grim nights in 1940, as bombs burst on the landscape above the War Rooms, Churchill could not envision May 8, 1945, when the Nazis would surrender, and he would stand on the balcony of Buckingham Palace with the royal family, celebrating the victory over the storm and commemorating the suffering.

The Lord Jesus Christ, in Matthew 24, warned His followers of the gathering storm of great tribulation, but He also talked about the proclamation of His kingdom reaching every nation and people group in the world. This would precede His return to earth at the climax of finite time.

Jesus described a massive harvest coming in the end times (Matt. 13). It will be the fruit of all the sowing of the gospel of the kingdom throughout the ages. It will be sudden, sweeping, and massive.

Through Paul, in 1 Corinthians 10, the Holy Spirit gave us a clue about when the end times begin. Everything that happened to Moses and the Hebrews during the Exodus and coming into the promised land "happened to them as an example, and they were written for our instruction, *upon whom the ends of the ages have come*" (1 Cor. 10:11, italics added).

Therefore, the Corinthian believers two thousand years ago were already living in the end times. Since the end times mark a crossing from the age of the law and the prophets into the age of grace, some things become clear. First, we are living in the period of the "birth pangs" (Matt. 24:8) immediately preceding His return. Second, we exist in the end times. Third, we should therefore expect a great revival ahead and prepare for it now.

There is evidence that revival has begun in the midst of the present storm of tribulation and intensifying immorality and paganism. Christians worldwide constitute an intensely persecuted group. Yet China, which was an impenetrable galaxy in my youth, is rapidly becoming one of the largest Christian populations in the world. Multitudes in the Middle East are turning to Christ. The demographic center of world Christianity has shifted to the Global South. Some of the largest churches in the British Isles have been planted by immigrants whose ancestors had been brought to Christ through the work of nineteenth-century missionaries from Britain.

In this book I focus on the Welsh Revival of 1904 because it is a foreshadowing of what the global revival ahead might look like.

We are now in the war rooms, at the core of the battle that rages above us and all around us. We cannot yet see the complete victory, but it is embedded in the storm!

Introduction

From about half past ten at night, to
about half after midnight, Fire!
—BLAISE PASCAL, 1654[1]

I was struck by a bolt of lightning many years ago that transformed my life and destiny.

It happened on a Friday night in July 1974.

After almost three years in the Washington swamp as a young aide in the Nixon White House, I was at last right in the center of God's will for my life. Six months earlier I had become pastor of a small church at the top of lovely Mobile Bay in Alabama. I had finally embraced the call God had given me at age fifteen to preach the gospel, a call I had run from for almost a decade.

There were ravenous beasts in the Washington swamp, and for most of my three years there I had walked gingerly around them lest I awaken them. But surprisingly I had come to a new understanding of God and His call on my life while working for the president who was about to be swallowed by the Leviathan of the Watergate scandals. I knew there also were vicious dragons and serpents in the church world I had entered, but I had the peace of knowing that God would sustain me through whatever came.

A major assault came that Friday night.

I was enjoying an evening at home with my family when the phone rang. The caller identified himself as a reporter with a national news syndicate. My blood chilled and I thought my heart would stop as he talked. There was a document before the House Judiciary Committee considering the impeachment of the president that seemed to suggest I might be implicated in some of the scandals related to the crisis that would ultimately make Richard Nixon the first president in American history to resign from office. I knew there was nothing there, but who would believe me?

I hung up, trembling. Harry Dent, my old boss at the White House, had told me as he left Washington there was a possibility the Watergate affair had been staged by the president's opponents to bring him down, along with everyone around him. There might be an attempt to create the appearance of guilt whether or not one had participated in Watergate and other political dirty tricks.

I wondered if I was about to be the target of a manufactured allegation. Reason told me it was unlikely. I had been a junior aide and not worth a lot of newspaper ink. Just how junior was clearly evident on the day Henry Kissinger made one of the most important announcements of the era—possible peace with Vietnam. Where was I? Escorting Colonel Harlan Sanders of fried chicken fame on a tour of the White House!

Reason, however, is squelched in situations of bare-knuckled fear pounding at your thoughts and emotions.

At about 9:30 that night I went out into the backyard and prayed. I awoke aching with anxiety the next morning after sleeping fitfully. The story broke, and media from around the country began to call. I realized that before our church members came to hear me preach the next morning, they would likely read in the *Mobile Press-Register* that I might have been involved somehow in the Watergate scandals.

LIGHTNING

I was dressed and ready for a Saturday evening engagement before my wife and children were, so I stretched out on our bed and wondered what to do about my situation. Suddenly I thought of Mrs. Chandler, a retired schoolteacher in our community who believed God had called her to pray for pastors. She had stopped by my office several times and prayed with me. I immediately phoned her.

"Mrs. Chandler," I said, "you are not going to believe what I am about to tell you." I then detailed what had happened.

"Let's pray," she said almost before I finished.

Mrs. Chandler prayed for me that Saturday afternoon on the telephone in a way I had never heard anyone pray before. It was not religious, not ritualistic, not formulaic. She was a woman really talking to God! There was binding and loosing and calling for the Holy Spirit to touch me. Without thinking about theology or religious correctness, I began to say over and again, "Yes, Lord, whatever she is praying for, yes! I agree, Lord!"

Suddenly—a word that so often pops up in the context of revival—I was struck. As I try to describe what happened I can only think of what the seventeenth-century philosopher-mathematician Blaise Pascal wrote in his diary the night the Holy Spirit filled him. He wrote only one word in his diary: *"Fire!"*[2]

My own word was *lightning*. You will understand why I chose to include that term in the title of this book. The Holy Spirit struck me that Saturday afternoon. Joy blasted into my being.

Laughter, peace, thanksgiving rocketed through me. My evangelical friends would call it the filling of the Spirit; my pentecostal and charismatic brothers and sisters would describe it as the baptism with the Spirit. Whatever the case, I was a man revived and transformed.

I am still full of the energy and the joy of that moment when the lightning bolt of personal revival struck me.

I never heard another word about Watergate. But the revival never stopped. I am seventy-five years old as I write these words, and that event is almost a half century in the past. And yet the strength and zeal I felt have not only lingered but increased.

Yes, increased! Even though without revival I would not know Christ as my Savior, would not know Him as Lord, would not know the manifestation of the Holy Spirit's baptism—and without revival I would not be writing these words—my passion for revival has intensified because I believe we are living in the end times and a great last-days revival is necessary before Jesus returns. That's why revival is more important to me than ever before and why I pen this book. Throughout its pages I will use the Welsh Revival of 1904 as a classic example of a genuine move of God that exhibited every category of revival revealed in the Bible, which I believe will be characteristics of the great last-days revival. We will learn what revival is, how it happens, and why it matters today more than at any other time in world history. We need such revival now—urgently—both for the renewal of the church and as a fulfillment of prophecy prior to Jesus' return.

If you are looking for signs of the end times, you don't have to look far. I believe the similarities in our present day to the time leading up to the Welsh Revival and the other crises that are at hand are revealing to us that we are in the early days of the great end-times outpouring of the Spirit. Nations are living under the threat of natural and man-made disasters. Radical Islam is seeking global domination. Abortion kills four thousand babies each day in America alone. Sexual immorality is reaching epic heights of depravity. Governments are becoming more tolerant of every kind of aberrant behavior. A new wave of theological confusion is systematically emerging in many of our churches. Compromise on once sacred biblical truths and practices is the "new" Christianity. The list goes on and on.

As I write these words, more than four decades have passed since that season of personal revival in the early 1970s. Yet I still feel its fire. My physical energy may be waning, but if anything, my spiritual zeal is intensifying. I understand better what the apostle Paul wrote as he aged and the intensity of the lightning that struck him on the Damascus Road still burned within: "Therefore we do not lose heart, but though our outer man is decaying, yet our inner man is being renewed day by day" (2 Cor. 4:16). And I see with more clarity what the prophet Joel prophesized: "In the last days, God says, I will pour out my Spirit on all people" (Acts 2:17 NIV).

In many ways I am a "child of revival"—as people impacted by the Welsh Revival in the early twentieth century referred to themselves. This is why writing this book means so much to me. All these years later, it still blazes deep within. I pray that God's lightning will energize your life as you read this book and that the church everywhere will be awakened to its true power in this crucial hour.

—WALLACE HENLEY

CHAPTER 1

We Need Lightning Now!

Can it happen again?
—LEWIS DRUMMOND[1]

I will never forget the lightning which came into his voice."
These words were uttered by Alun Morgan of Caerfarchell, a man who experienced the Welsh Revival of 1904. The memory was voiced to friends in the 1930s, more than two decades after Morgan had heard Evan Roberts speak.

Yet Morgan had never forgotten the lightning that character-ized Roberts in those years.[2]

When the revival bolt hit Evan Roberts, a church leader described the young man as "acting like a particle of radium" or a "consuming fire which took away sleep, cleared the channels of tears and sped the wheels of prayer throughout this district."[3]

Evan himself would never forget the spiritual bolt that struck him. A few weeks later he told W. T. Stead, a journalist, that it was

"Living Energy." It had "invaded his soul, burst all bonds, and overwhelmed him."[4]

The lightning struck Roberts during a September 29, 1904, service conducted by Seth Joshua at Blaenannerch. The first meeting had been at seven that morning. During that session, Evan began to sense an "irresistible influence" coming upon him as he heard Joshua pray, "Bend me!"

Evan had trundled the road from Newcastle Emlyn to Blaenannerch in a wagon with Joshua and a group of fellow students. All the way there Evan had felt confused, swinging from gloom to joy. But there was something in the "Bend me" prayer that resonated deeply within him.

After that early meeting and before the next, which would be at 9:00 a.m., Evan and his friends and Joshua breakfasted at the home of Pastor M. P. Morgan. Later, journeying to the chapel, Joshua spoke suddenly: "We are going to have a wonderful meeting here today." Evan answered, "I am just bursting!"

During the 9:00 a.m. service, Evan sat in a pew off to the side with friends from Newquay. Evan was struggling. He remembered that a little earlier, at breakfast, Magdalen Phillips had passed him bread and butter, and he had refused it. As he had watched Joshua receive the same food, a thought sliced into Evan's psyche: *What if God offers His Spirit, and I am not ready to receive Him, and others are ready to accept Him were they offered?*[5]

This angst stirred in Evan as he sat in the Blaenannerch chapel. It was so evident that two ministers took note of the anguished young man and concluded he was neurotic.

But the ground of Evan's soul was experiencing the buildup of the charge. Within moments the revival lightning struck him.

At the start of the meeting, many were praying.

"Shall I pray now?" Evan asked the Lord.

"No," he sensed the Holy Spirit saying.

Evan obeyed and sat in silence. In that interval the charge continued to intensify in his spirit and soul. The cloud of God's manifest presence seemed to hover over him. Finally, as Evan waited and others around him prayed, he felt the "living energy." He trembled as the energy built up within him.

"Shall I pray now?" Evan asked the Holy Spirit. He felt that he would explode if he didn't speak out in prayer. Evan then entered into the "Bend me" prayer, and the lightning struck with intensity. Later he described it:

> What boiled in my bosom was the verse, "For God commendeth His love." I fell on my knees with my arms outstretched on the seat before me. The perspiration poured down my face and my tears streamed quickly until I thought the blood came out. Mrs. Davies of Mona, Newquay, came to wipe my face, and Magdalen Phillips stood on my right and Maud Davies on my left. I cried, "Bend Me, Bend Me, Bend Me . . . OH! OH! OH!" Mrs. Davies said, "O wonderful grace." "Yes," said I, "O wonderful grace." It was God commending His love that bent me, and I not seeing anything to commend. After I was "bended," a wave of peace and joy filled my bosom.[6]

In a short time the humble youth, a gangly former coal miner, would-be blacksmith, and student preparing for seminary would be regarded as the leader of the 1904 Revival and remembered that way by history. Lightning is thus an apt metaphor for spiritual revival. When the Holy Spirit's power strikes, the flesh is seared through conviction and experiences "death," while the face is turned toward heaven, from whence came the bolt.

"The revival would usually come suddenly, and people could name the day and the hour that this happened," wrote Welsh historian R. Tudur Jones. They would use descriptive terms like "as the floodgates opened" or "the fire came down" or "the baptism happened."[7] *Suddenly* was a much-used word by those who would be touched by the revival.

Sometimes it takes a bolt of lightning to get our attention. In our time we have come to the point that we must have revival as dramatic, searing, and life-giving as that bolt that singed Martin Luther's soul and sent his body diving to the ground.

All other solutions have failed us. We must have the bolt of revival or perish. We must have the bolt of revival as a precursor to our Lord's return. And when I say we need revival, and that there is little hope in anything else, I feel both the words and the urgency.

I am not alone.

Fraying Society

In a *New York Times* article, Roger Cohen put our situation into stark perspective. He imagined a future conversation about the grim situations of the present: "It was the time of unraveling . . . beheadings . . . aggression . . . breakup . . . weakness . . . hatred . . . fever . . . disorientation." Cohen explained:

> The fabric of society frayed. Democracy looked quaint or outmoded beside new authoritarianisms. Politicians, haunted by their incapacity, played on the fears of their populations, who were device-distracted or under device-driven stress. Dystopia

was a vogue word, like utopia in the 20th century. The great rising nations of vast populations held the fate of the world in their hands but hardly seemed to care. . . .

Until it was too late and people could see the Great Unraveling for what it was and what it had wrought.[8]

This "great unraveling" is a result of our soul being sick because it is broken. When Adam and Eve rebelled, evil sundered the soul from the spirit. We are fragmented beings. The spirit died to God, and there was nothing transcendent to guide thoughts, emotions, choices, and thus the deeds done in the body.

This can no longer be dismissed as the outmoded thinking of religious fanatics. The madness around us is proof.

Can we not see it? How blind can we be?

Revival returns God to the human spirit through the Holy Spirit, whose fruit is love, joy, peace, patience, kindness, goodness, faithfulness, gentleness, and self-control (Gal. 5:22–23). What's wrong with that? "Plenty," say elitist establishments who have given us all the other balms and plans and theories that are supposed to heal us but only make us sicker.

Revival links the Spirit-indwelt human spirit with the soul once again, as in the days when Eden was called Paradise.

Before that, it was a *tohubohu*—formless and void, chaotic and barren. Then the Holy Spirit brooded over the face of the deep and Paradise emerged. Revival, as we will see, is the Holy Spirit brooding over us again, nurturing true life, connecting us to God, enabling us to experience at least a touch of the paradise that will come again at the coming again of the creative Logos without whom nothing was made that was made: the Lord Jesus Christ.

The Stakes Are Higher Now

The stakes are higher at this hour than at any other time in world history. In the nuclear buildups of the Cold War era, under the doctrine of mutually assured destruction, a grim possibility emerged that history had never before faced: humanity possessed enough firepower to wipe out the whole world. The Cold War opponents understood that, and the possibility of their own destruction held them at bay.

But as I write, we are in a season of delusion and madness. Nuclear power is in the hands of tyrants who have little concern for anything but themselves and the authoritarian control to which they cling. Some believe global destruction works into their apocalyptic vision and mission. Others care little for the retaliation that might fall on their own people as long as they can emerge from their secure, luxurious bunkers to preside as the hegemons over empires of rubble and smoke.

What we need is revival of the scope and power of that which struck the British principality of Wales in 1904. What happened was a dramatic, sudden interaction between heaven and earth as a mighty cloud of revival passed over and released its energy upon the little region. I believe such a revival is near at hand.

F. B. Meyer was intimately involved in the Welsh Revival and summed it up: "Judging by the fruits, in the vast multitude who have been truly converted and have joined the churches, and the transformation wrought over wide districts of the country, it is impossible to doubt that there has been a real and deep work by the Spirit of God, similar to that which accompanied the labours of the Wesleys and their contemporaries."[9]

David Matthews concluded in the midst of his encounters with the revival that "sacred and secular history prove that a glorious outpouring of the Spirit of God can so completely change the current of human thought as to make men and women almost unrecognizable to their companions of former days."[10] In fact, H. Elvet Lewis, another revival participant, wrote in 1906 that Wales's "entire history . . . has been reshaped by it."[11]

What was "it"? History calls it the Welsh Revival of 1904, but Lewis was reminded of the label Simon Peter gave to the empowering, transforming move of God on the Day of Pentecost: "This is what was spoken of through the prophet Joel" (Acts 2:16).

"The apostle of Pentecost had to be content with this one syllable—*This*," wrote Lewis, in the wake of the lightning that struck the land—and his own life. Looking back to the momentous events through which he had lived and that still burned within him, Lewis wrote: "Out of all of this shines *This*—nameless, mystic, all-subduing. Dates, places, and persons were only outward and visible symbols of a wave—more, a tide—nay, an overwhelming flood, that has no everyday name, no secular explanation. . . . There was no name for it, only the equation of an old and hallowed memory. It was *This*."[12]

IMAGINE

In his song, "Imagine," John Lennon beckoned us to imagine a world without heaven, countries, possessions, and especially without religion. But imagine a world *with* not mere religion but true heavenly revival impacting every facet of human life and engagement on earth.

What would *this* look like if let loose in the world? What will *this* look like in the coming end-times revival?

God gave us a glimpse in 1904 in Wales. Something happened that still defies attempts at explanation, apart from an act of God

Himself, over several months in the early twentieth century in that slice of land sandwiched between England and the Irish Sea. A close examination of the Welsh Revival of 1904 shows what the world would look like if the carcass of moribund religion was struck by the very energy of God—no imagining needed.

Consider this sampling:[13]

- Within eight months of the Welsh Revival, more than 100,000 people had joined churches, with 70,000 turning to Christ in the first two months. As I write this, the population of the United States is about 325 million. If what happened in Wales in 1904–1905 happened in modern America, it would mean that 30 million people would commit their lives to Christ in a six-to-eight-month period.

- David Matthews, a participant in the revival of 1904–1905 said that eight months after its outbreak, 150,000 had joined Welsh churches.

   "It is a fact that large numbers have been *added to the Churches*. Not merely converted or restored, or helped on, but become full members. . . . It is a significant fact that in one corner of South Wales, in one denomination alone, between 6,000 and 7,000 new members were added during two or three months."

   "That which costly legislation, cumbersome philanthropic effort, organizations and associations have failed to do, here the Spirit of God is doing with an ease and thoroughness surprising to behold. Drunkards give up drinking without pledge or pressure. Quarrels are healed without 'the courts.' Homes made happy. . . . Debts paid without legislation. Streets purified without threat or fine. . . . The quest for holiness became the passion of the man in the street."

Matthews also reported that every pub in Llanfair in Anglesey was closed.

Welsh newspapers carried statistics reporting increases in church attendance, especially among miners and others working in blue-collar trades. Then reports linked the uptick in church attendance by working people to a surge in industrial output and the economy, which, said Matthews, "spiraled up unbelievably."

"Criminal calendars were reduced to a minimum. . . . Lists of convictions dwindled to nothing," Matthews observed. Judges, instead of facing loaded dockets, stared at blank pages. They were given white gloves, a rarely used symbol of clean dockets going all the way back to the beginnings of the British legal system.

This was evidenced in "Statistics from Chief Constable's Office," Canton, Cardiff, for the number of convictions for drunkenness in the county, dated November 10, 1908, and affirmed by chief clerk Alfred Thomas:

1902: 9,298
1903: 10,528
1904: 10,282
1905: 8,164
1906: 5,490
1907: 5,615

+ "Hundreds of homes have been entirely changed, and where there were poverty and misery before, there is plenty of all the necessities of life now, and happiness," noted D. M. Phillips in his biography of Evan Roberts. Further, he said, "The Revival has changed the whole moral and spiritual aspects of many districts, and its future effects must be great."[14]

+ "Men who had been regarded as either too old or too wicked to be touched and saved, surrendered fully and absolutely, and have since become useful citizens and consistent church members," noted J. Vynrwy Morgan.[15] The fact that Morgan was something of a critic of the Revival, and Evan Roberts especially, lends even more credence to the amazing reports of the revival's impact.

+ F. B. Meyer wrote: "Judging from the fruits, in the vast multitude who have been truly converted and have joined the churches, and the transformation wrought over wide districts of the country, it is impossible to doubt that there has been a real and deep work by the Spirit of God."[16]

+ Family worship was started or restored in thousands of homes.

+ Booksellers could not keep up with the demand for Bibles.

+ More people embraced total abstinence from alcohol.

+ Hundreds paid debts, even those canceled by the statute of limitations.

+ People were surprised when money suddenly showed up from thieves who had stolen goods from them as many as twenty years earlier, and the payment was in full and with interest.

+ Family and church conflicts were settled by the hundreds.

+ Churches pulsated with joy as people experienced overwhelming strength through the Holy Spirit.

+ Different church groups and denominations, though still organizationally separated, came together in new manifestations of spiritual fellowship.

+ Churches suddenly had new workers for their ministries. These included former agnostics and infidels, boxers and other athletes, town and village drunks, entertainers, and others who previously disdained or took no thought of church, let alone volunteering in ministries.

- Morality and ethics were elevated to a higher level throughout entire districts of Wales.
- A Cardiff newspaper observed: "Many who have disbelieved Christianity for years are again returning to the fold of their younger days."[17]
- Football stadiums and theaters closed their doors for lack of customers.
- Political events shut down because people rallied instead at churches.
- Vice-based businesses were shuttered.
- Dying churches on the verge of disbanding were now packed.
- Men once known for their profanity became eloquent intercessors.
- Formality in worship was replaced by a Spirit-inspired outflow of passionate expression in song, testimony, and prayer.
- Homes that had lacked spiritual leadership and whose walls had echoed with blaspheming and cursing now were filled with reverence and praise.
- Wales was famous for its great soloists, many of whom traveled across the principality singing God's praise because they simply could not withhold their new passion for Him.
- Newspapers reported an entire football team had turned to Christ and conversion had become so common that games were canceled.
- Dance halls in several places were devoid of music and partygoers.
- People were breaking out in testimony in marketplaces, street corners, and town squares, telling how the Lord had transformed their lives.
- Railway platforms and trains were filled with hymn singing, prayer, and witness.

- A man at a public meeting thanked God that not only could Jesus Christ, the Savior, "turn water into wine, but that He had turned beer into furniture in his home," while his wife listened, and clapped, and wiped tears from her eyes.
- The Cardiff newspaper *Western Mail* reported on November 10, 1904: "Shopkeepers are closing earlier in order to get a place in the chapel, and tin and steel workers throng the place in their working clothes."
- "Perhaps the greatest wonder was the transforming effect that the revival produced upon the minds and conduct of the coal miners," but what happened in Wales "had its effect even on these dumb animals"—the pit ponies that pulled the coal-laden carriages up from the mines had to be retrained to respond to commands without profanity and blasphemy. Said a man at Cardiff: "The people, Lord, do not understand the strange things that are happening, neither to the horses that are down in the pit."[18] A mine manager told theologian and preacher G. Campbell Morgan: "The haulers are some of the lowest [men]. They have driven their horses by obscenity and kicks. Now they can hardly persuade their horses to start working, because there is no obscenity and no kicks."[19]

End-Times Revival Results

The great end-times revival will have the same results. It will have the *This* that H. Elvet Lewis wrote about. It will be a God-sent, Holy Spirit–ignited revival that brings people to their knees, not in protest, but in affirmation of the Lord of lords and King of kings. He is the only power who can bring life back to our spirit and heal sickened, demonized psyches by linking revived spirits with souls and who will soon be seen by all mankind as the apostle John described:

> "Look, he is coming with the clouds,"
>   and "every eye will see him,
> even those who pierced him";
>   and all peoples on earth "will mourn because of him."
>   So shall it be! Amen. (Rev. 1:7 NIV)

Almost exactly four centuries before the spiritual lightning struck Evan Roberts, an actual bolt jarred a young German who was sauntering toward the Saxon village of Stotternheim. That day in 1505 was shrouded by angry clouds. Suddenly a bolt of lightning rocketed downward, striking near the stocky man. It interrupted his thoughts and hurled him to the ground, terrified.

"Saint Anne, help me! I will become a monk!" cried Martin Luther.

There can be no doubt that the bolt got Martin Luther's attention that day and changed his life. He would never forget it or the lessons he learned from the lightning. "When lightning strikes a tree or a man, it does two things at once—it rends the tree and swiftly slays the man. But it also turns the face of the dead man and broken branches of the tree itself toward heaven,"[20] Luther later wrote.

We must call down the lightning. We don't have to cajole God into sending it. His great heart pulsates with the desire to renew us and our societies. In fact, there is a historical cycle in which revival recurs across time. A cycle that will culminate in the revival to end all revivals—the great last-days revival!

The good news is that as we study that cycle, we discover that contemporary nations are ripe for the lightning of this final outpouring!

CHAPTER 2

The Times and Seasons of True Revival

There is an appointed time for everything. And there is a time for every event under heaven—

—ECCLESIASTES 3:1

According to an old song, April showers bring May flowers. So when the April rains come, they are actually pouring down violets.

But a farmer in Israel contemplating the end of April and the coming of May might not have such an optimistic view. For him, May signals the end of the rainy season and the beginning of a stretch of drought extending into October, when intermittent showers start, known in the Bible as the early rain. He knows gales will blow down from the far north from December through February. Then will come the latter rains, which will nourish the seed plowed into the ground during the season of early rain.

So when April gives way to May, this rugged farmer thinks of the arid stretch ahead. Dust storms will swirl like locusts. Cracks will sketch out the agony of the water-starved face of the landscape. Searing dry heat will wrap everything in its suffocating grip. The Sea of Galilee will be watched by nervous monitors who know the water that keeps the nation alive springs from this great basin. They will survey for the slightest evidences of drought, which can be deadly. The land, the animals, and the people will yearn for the early rain, the former rain, and the latter rain.

In the Middle East and most other areas around the world, there can be spotty, intermittent showers at almost any time. But many nations depend on seasonal rain—the monsoons. Without the monsoon season, survival is impossible in such places. So the prophetic words God gave Joel brought great encouragement to the Hebrews: "[God] will cause to come down for you the rain, the former rain, and the latter rain in the first month" (Joel 2:23 KJV).

Such is the nature of revival. It is not a random event but an entire season.

DROUGHT ON A TEXAS RANCH

My wife and I once owned a ranch seventy miles northwest of Houston, in the foothills of the Texas Hill Country. Cattle grazed its verdant fields and slaked their thirst with big gulps from a large pond (called a "tank" in Texas). One spring we and other ranchers awoke to the fact there had been no significant rain for weeks. A drought set in. I watched anxiously as the tank shrank until it was a mud pit and then a dry gulch. The green grass turned deathly gray. Rolls of hay that normally cost $40 now sold for $140.

One day a little shower swept over the property. Hope rose in our hearts, but swift winds blew it away. The situation became so desperate that some people even wished for a hurricane. Though it was the tropical storm season, the Atlantic and the Gulf of Mexico remained quiet.

We needed a season of rain. Eventually it came, and with it a great lesson: Don't mistake a brief shower for a monsoon. Spiritually there are outbreaks here and sprinklings there, and we believe revival at last has come. We are satisfied with droplets when we need a drenching. We stop praying for revival, preparing for it, searching the horizons of heaven for it, and go back to our dry religious landscapes.

Wales had seen intermittent spiritual showers many times. "There are traces of the action of revivals in Wales from the first appearance of Christianity here," wrote H. Elvet Lewis. Revival in Wales, he said, "reappears time after time."[1] At special times those intermittent showers linked to become regional revivals. The merging of the rains became a monsoon. "The seventeenth century was a period of expansion and consolidation for the gospel," wrote Eifion Evans. Welsh churches in the seventeenth century and again in the nineteenth, he said, "experienced times of decline and inactivity interspersed with revival periods of vigorous energy and spiritual prosperity." However, Evans noted, they were "mainly localized."[2] Leaders were notables in their region: Richard Baxter, Robert Murray McCheyne, and David Morgan.

Eifion Evans thought the 1830s to be "the most exciting decade in modern history," because "God graciously visited America, England, Scotland and Wales with powerful revivals." At first they were intermittent and localized, but eventually they linked and became a monsoon of revival. In just a few years "they were fused into one mighty awakening, when whole countries and vast tracts of land were submerged in a surge of divine power and momentous spiritual upheaval."[3]

Leading up to the spiritual monsoon of 1904–1905 in Wales, Aberyswth had been sprinkled upon in 1805, Beddgelert in 1817, Anglesey in 1822, Carmarthen in 1828, and Merioneth in 1840, to name a few.[4] These were, however, local and failed to refresh the whole principality. Such a powerful move of God came in 1859, but it, too, eventually faded. As the nineteenth century neared its end, however, church leaders tended to be caught up in movements ranging from temperance and cultural reform to depriving individuals of the status and privileges of the established church, that is, the Church of England. All these seemed to be a religious version of the progressive impulse of the Victorian era. "These were worthy causes, but absorbed the time, energy, and talents of the finest men and women in the churches so that direct evangelism, holiness and the personal knowledge of God were neglected," wrote Welsh historian David R. J. Ollerton.[5] This resulted, he said, "in a spiritual vacuum in the churches."

Wales is not like the Middle Eastern lands or the geographies of Asia that depend on actual monsoon seasons, but it did become a place of spiritual monsoons. Not only was it known as "the Land of Song" but also "the Land of Revivals," said David Matthews, an observer and participant in the Welsh Revival of 1904. When they looked back from the perspective of 1906 to the seventeenth century, Matthews and other students of Welsh history saw the principality had experienced significant revival about every ten years.[6]

"It would be misleading to claim that these small-scale, local movements of the Holy Spirit had any significant and lasting influence in the background to the revival of 1904," noted Eifion Evans. "Nevertheless at a time of almost general declension they did keep alive in the minds, as well as the hearts, of the people of God the divine pattern for carrying forward the work of His Kingdom."[7]

The twentieth century burst upon the industrialized nations like a supernova. Victorian romanticism conjoined with Enlightenment rationalism, and the public's focus was on great progressivist advances. Yet Christian leaders in Wales were conscious of the decline of spiritual life in the principality even as humanistic optimism increased. The result was a new wave of prayer for true revival. God's answer came in the spiritual monsoon of 1904–1905.

The Times and the Seasons

There is a law of periodicity regarding movements, including revivals, wrote Lewis Drummond, an authority on the history and nature of revivals. "History is full of instances where churches have felt a desperate need for revival only to experience little blessing. Then when least expected, the heavens opened." By using the word *law*, Drummond was not speaking in terms of legalism, because, as he noted, the Spirit moves as He wills. But *periodicity* as it relates to revival works on "the basis of the inscrutable hidden purposes of God" and it reveals three important facts:

- "God is in control of His church and will give His people what they need when they need it."
- "God's wisdom far supersedes ours, and we must place the timing of these awakenings in the divine economy of things."
- "Revivals do not come by caprice or just because the church does certain things in a formal, structured fashion, [though]

the people of God do have a part, [but] the sovereignty of God is central."[8]

Revival is part of a cycle revealed in God's interactions with the prototypical nation (Old Testament Israel), and the experience of Wales shows this. "As in the Book of Judges, so in the history of this little nation, God raised up men of inflexible conviction and great audacity," wrote David Matthews.[9] They appeared at different times on the human calendar, but they were part of the spiritual monsoon seasons that refreshed Wales throughout the decades in which they served. So it will also be in the days of the great end-times revival, as men and women of extraordinary spiritual and leadership gifts will be raised up.

In fact, the Bible tells of times and seasons, and it is important to recognize the differences between the two lest we miss the coming sovereign move of God.

Every belief system, whether it's secular materialism or religious mysticism, develops a theory of time. Western thought tends to see time as strictly linear, moving from beginning to termination, from past to present to future. Oriental philosophies, influenced by Hinduism and other nirvana religions, view time as cyclical, moving in an endlessly repeating circle rather than a straight line.

The Bible shows the reality of time as both linear (*kronos*) and cyclical (*kairos*). This is not as impossible as it sounds. Think of a train moving along a track: there is linear progression toward the destination, but the train is carried along by the cyclical, repeating motion of the wheels. The linear-cyclical view is expressed well by Solomon: "What is happening now has happened before, and what will happen in the future has happened before, because God makes the same things happen over and over again" (Eccl. 3:15 NLT).

Encounter with Time

We see this linkage of the linear-cyclical dynamic of time in both the Old and New Testaments, the Hebrew Bible and the Greek Bible.

I have labeled *kairos* time as K^1 and *kronos* time as K^2. This junction of the two qualities of time is expressed in the New Testament by the phrase "the fullness of time." In the Old Testament, the arrival of Israel's feast seasons in the chronological calendar constituted the fullness of time. In the New Testament, the arrival in chronological time of the reality to which the feasts of Israel pointed is the fullness of time.

The imagery is very different. "Fullness" comes from the Greek word *pleroma*, which is seen graphically in the filling of a cup to the rim. Chronological time drips in seconds, minutes, hours, days, weeks, months, and years until the cup of history reaches a degree of fullness.

Every event celebrated in the Old Testament looked forward to one thing: the coming of the Messiah. Therefore, Paul wrote, "When the fullness of the time came, God sent forth His Son, born of a woman, born under the Law" (Gal. 4:4). The Son exists eternally with the Father and is therefore a remarkable *kairos* (K^1) person who becomes incarnate in *kronos* (K^2 sequence). The Christological equation is thus $K^1 + K^2 =$ Jesus, the Christ. The Lord Jesus Christ is therefore the singularity from which all else comes and by which all is upheld (John 1:1, 14; Col. 1:17; Heb. 1:3).

Order Amid Chaos

Revival has sustained God's order amid the chaos of fallen nations since Pentecost. The last great revival will prepare the world for

Jesus' step back into *kronos* time and bring the rule of His kingdom of "righteousness, peace and joy in the Holy Spirit" (Rom. 14:17 NIV) as the state of the whole redeemed creation.

Thus it should not surprise us that the cloud of God's presence in the form of revival appears at crucial intervals across history and will again at the end of history. *Kronos* events will be cycling over and again on the linear track when suddenly *kairos* intervenes in space-time. All the history since Christ's ascension will have reached its fullness.

To put it another way, the wave of revival will have to be at its crest.

CHAPTER 3

The Revival Cycle

Will You not Yourself revive us again,
That Your people may rejoice in You?

—PSALM 85:6

There is a principle of the ebb and flow of revival, Tom Phillips wrote. Any spiritual advance in the human relationship with God is "like the incoming tide," with every wave "a revival, going forward, receding, and being followed by another," James Burns said, as cited by Phillips. "To the onlooker, it seems as if nothing is gained, but the force behind the ebb and flow is the power of the tide."[1] Learning how to recognize the signs of the final great tidal wave of revival is critical for our preparation and participation.

There is therefore a wave action, as Burns and Phillips suggest, or a sequence to revival. The pattern emerges in a careful study of Judges and other scriptures.[2]

RATIFICATION

Ratification in the sense it is used here refers to a period when the people of a nation, their government, and other institutions are in a state of consensus about their core beliefs and their principles.

We see an era of ratification in Old Testament Israel during the glorious age of Joshua, who had inherited from Moses the idea that God was to be at the center of their civilization. This vital understanding had to be passed on to the children. As long as there was ratification of that consensus among the leadership and the people, Israel flourished. While Joshua was alive, he kept the centrality of God before his people. Among Joshua's last acts was to establish a binding covenant around that central vision of God at the core of culture and then to record the decision in the Book of the Law of God, the "constitution" of the Hebrew nation.

This period of ratification of God's centrality in Old Testament Israel led to a season of rest. The Hebrews then passed through periods when they forgot God and rebelled against Him and His ways. They would repent and again ratify the covenant that recognized God as the core of their lives and culture—until they lapsed again.

RELAPSE

Old Testament Israel's ratification consensus around God collapsed when Joshua and his generation passed. Ultimately, "there arose another generation after them who did not know the LORD, nor yet the work which He had done for Israel" (Judg. 2:10).

Aleksandr Solzhenitsyn's eye-opening speech in 1983 should haunt us now. The great Russian writer, philosopher, dissident, and Orthodox Christian was exiled from his native land. Born in 1918, a year after the Bolshevik Revolution put the communists in control in Russia, Solzhenitsyn had seen into the core of communism's dark heart and tried to warn his nation about the atheism that would facilitate widespread atrocities. For that, Solzhenitsyn was charged with crimes against the state and spent years in the Gulag, the infamous Siberian prisons he described in several books, starting with *The Gulag Archipelago*. In 1974 he was charged with treason and stripped of his citizenship—which was restored in 1990 after communism collapsed and the Soviet Union disintegrated.

Solzhenitsyn loved his country and wanted desperately to understand what had happened to it. On May 9, 1983, he described it to an audience in London when he received the Templeton Prize for Progress in Religion. "Over a half century ago, while I was still a child, I recall hearing a number of old people offer the following explanation for the great disasters that have befallen Russia: 'Men have forgotten God; that's why all this has happened.'"[3]

Eifion Evans, the Welsh historian with a passion for revival whom we have quoted extensively in chapter 2, would have understood the grief of the old Russians to whom Solzhenitsyn referred. Evans was born in 1931 and died at the age of eighty-six on November 1, 2017. He had studied the fifteen or more revivals that had swept across Wales since Reformation times. He rejoiced as he wrote of the great moves of God in the eighteenth century, which he said was "one continuous flow of revivals."[4] He was intimately acquainted with the 1904 revival. He was old enough to have felt some of the warmth still radiating from that move of God and yet young enough to live in the spiritually barren eras of the twentieth and twenty-first centuries. He was thus acutely aware of the relapse of the communal memory of God's great work in his land in modern times.

REBELLION

Again Old Testament Israel is an example. We saw above how, when Joshua and his generation died, Israel's memory relapsed and the people forgot God and the God-centered principles given to them by their founders. At some point after Joshua and his generation passed off the scene, and as men and women increasingly forgot God and His centrality in the formation of their nation, rebellion intensified.

REFINER'S FIRE

The refiner's fire is the manifestation in society of its rebellion from God and His ways. In the Old Testament, the passing of Joshua and his generation provides an example and context in which the refiner's fire came to Israel. It led to a period when the Hebrew people forgot God as the core of their nation and then went into outright rebellion. Then "the anger of the LORD burned against Israel" (2 Sam. 24:1), but as subsequent events showed, this was not simply punitive judgment but rather fires of purification.

The refiner's fire comes as the consequences of rebellion fall on society. The ruins of the great institutions that had stabilized the nation—in ancient Israel's case, the Torah and the center of worship, family life, learning, governance, and work arising from it—became kindling for the conflagration that seared and melted the nation.

Through the prophet Zechariah, the Holy Spirit gave us a fascinating insight into the nature of God's refining work:

> "It will come about in all the land,"
> Declares the LORD,

"That two parts in it will be cut off and perish;
But the third will be left in it.
And I will bring the third part through the fire,
Refine them as silver is refined,
And test them as gold is tested.
They will call on My name,
And I will answer them;
I will say, 'They are My people,'
And they will say, 'The LORD is my God.'" (Zech. 13:8–9)

The aim of the refiner's fire on the nation is to burn away the dross so the precious metal—silver or gold in the prophetic analogy—is all that is left. In the case of the nation, this third that endures and is purified through the refining fire is the remnant, the people who remain faithful to God during the stage of rebellion and who refuse to join in.

What happened to Israel reveals the nature of this judgment.

+ God gave them into the hands of plunderers who plundered them.

    The plundering of the church comes as some reject the Bible as authoritative and abandon sound doctrine. The plunderer is culture. Because the apostate church has abandoned its core, it is easily overwhelmed by cultural propaganda and trends. This is the type of church described as having "itching ears" (2 Tim. 4:3 NIV). The spiritually and doctrinally plundered church is the Laodicean church of Revelation 3:14–22.

    The apostasy pours over into culture. Charles Colson wrote,

    I believe that today in the West and particularly in America, the new barbarians are all around us. They are not hairy Goths and Vandals, swilling fermented brew and ravishing maidens; they are not Huns and Visigoths storming our borders or scaling our city walls. No, this time the invaders have come from within. We have bred them in our families and trained them in our classrooms. They inhabit our legislatures, our courts, our film studios, and our churches. Most of them are attractive and pleasant; their ideas are persuasive and subtle. Yet these men and women threaten our most cherished institutions and our very character as a people.[5]

+ God sold them into the hands of their enemies and they could no longer stand before their enemies.

The idea of God selling out the rebellious Israelites seems callous and offensive. Obviously, the idea of God getting value for Himself from the enemies of the Hebrews is not the point of this text. Rather it's the idea of disposing of a property in which there is no longer a possibility of relationship and meaning for the seller.

Israel once belonged to God. The Israelites walked in a special covenant with Him. That relationship was loaded with benefits. Prior to entering the promised land, Moses had laid out the options with blunt clarity. He spoke of the curses that would fall on the nation if it walked away from its covenant with God and the blessings the Hebrews would enjoy if they continued as covenant walkers.

+ Wherever they went, the hand of the LORD was against them for evil (Judg. 2:15).

Something terrible happened between the battles at Jericho and Ai. Jericho fell before the Hebrew warriors with the blasts of trumpets and shouts. Yet Ai, a much smaller and less defended city, seemed unconquerable. The problem, Joshua discovered, was the violation by one of his soldiers of the command God had laid down regarding the spoils of battle.

God had stipulated that everything left in Jericho should be devoted to Him. Achan, however, couldn't resist taking a Babylonian garment he found in the ruins. Why would this make God set His hand against Israel in the battle at Ai? The answer is that, because of the violation of God's command, the whole nation was in a state of hostility against God. A brief look at some scriptures helps us understand the seriousness of this and how it brings on the refiner's fire. The Bible specifies those whom God actively opposes or with whom He is in a state of enmity or war.

God actively opposes the proud (James 4:6). Human arrogance is terribly destructive and infects whole nations. Some wonder why the whole nation had to suffer because of Achan's sin. The truth is that evil is like cancer: it begins in the rebellion of one cell and soon spreads. The only way Israel could stand against the giants in the land was through God's power. Pride would have brought their total destruction. Better to lose a small battle at Ai and learn the lesson than be defeated in the war.

The whole experience prodded some among the Hebrews to wonder what they had left behind.

REMEMBRANCE

The prophet Malachi described one of these early remembrance periods in Old Testament Israel and Judah: "They that feared the Lord spake often one to another: and the LORD hearkened, and heard it, and a book of remembrance was written before him for them that feared the Lord, and that thought upon his name" (Mal. 3:16 kjv).

As several Bible scholars have pointed out, the Hebrew word *zakar*, meaning "remember," always has action attached to it. When people recalled the treasures of the past, they began to recover them. The prophets then connected the dots between the past and the present. And they went further, showing outcomes for the future if there was not a return to the old values and to the core of God's revealed truth for the nation.

The prophets arose in the age of remembrance, calling the people back to the God they had forgotten and His ways. But at first the prophets were rejected. One of those who remembered and sought to call the people to remembrance was Howell Harris, one of those prophetic men in eighteenth-century Wales.

On a 1740 visit to North Wales, Harris grieved "over the darkness, superstition, and immorality which characterized the land," wrote Eifion Evans.[6] Harris mourned the state of the people that had resulted from the eras of rebellion and its consequences. "This country is ruined for want of experimental [experiential] preaching of Christ powerfully," Harris lamented. There "was no gospel light but in a few places."[7]

The more Harris saw, the more he grieved. "O Lord, I can't help mourning over the darkness of the country of North Wales! North Wales! Thy guides are blind, the magistrates are persecutors, and the instruments for Thee are all weak." He could find only a few godly men here and there in all of North Wales.

Harris and a few others began to cry out wherever they could, urging the people to return to God. They understood how the blind guides were leading deluded people over a spiritual cliff. False teaching permeated the churches. But men like Harris tried to bring the restoration of solid biblical truth, and they paid the price. Eifion Evans observed:

> For their uncompromising stand with regard to these matters and because they sought to lead the nation, the clergy, and the Church back to New Testament principles and practices, they were often excluded from the churches by their enemies, persecuted by the mobs, and attacked in the pamphlets and printed works of the time.[8]

Yet they persisted, and at last others began to awaken and remember what they had forgotten and lost. Slowly, people began coming back to churches, being truly born again. Soon they were forming fellowship groups, where they prayed for one another and their land. "There could be only one explanation for these phenomena," said Evans, and that was the fact that "God had visited the land in a tremendous outpouring of His Spirit and of power, making that to blossom as the rose which had been formerly a desolated wilderness."[9]

REPENTANCE

The book of Judges reveals, for example, how during a phase of rebellion Israel "did evil" in God's sight. The refiner's fire period occurred then as "the LORD gave them into the hands of Midian seven years" (Judg. 6:1). The Hebrews suffered terribly under their cruel enemy, and many had to abandon their homes and seek shelter in caves, mountain dens, and strongholds. "So Israel was brought very low because of Midian" (Judg. 6:6). This prompted the sons of Israel to cry out to the Lord. In response, He sent them a prophet to remind them of how God had cared for the nation historically, and He sent Gideon to deliver the Hebrews from the Midianites.

How does the United States or any nation repent? They do so in the same way ancient Israel carried out national repentance: through a faithful remnant.

This principle is apparent at the dedication of Solomon's temple. God promises,

> [If] My people who are called by My name humble themselves and pray and seek My face and turn from their wicked ways, then I will hear from heaven, will forgive their sin and will heal their land. Now My eyes will be open and My ears attentive to the prayer offered in this place. For now I have chosen and consecrated this house that My name may be there forever, and My eyes and My heart will be there perpetually. (2 Chron. 7:14–16)

We will explore this great promise in greater detail in chapter 7; however, "judgment is to begin with God's household" (1 Peter 4:17 NIV). National repentance begins with repentance in the church.

Evan Roberts understood this. It is tempting to try to make revival happen by formula and sustain it by legalism. Formulas and legalistic procedures emerge when we try to strategize a movement of God. Yet Evan concluded there were four points that must guide people in their hope for revival. These four principles came to him not through an effort to develop a flowchart or a blueprint for revival, but in the arena of action—as God's anointing for revival leadership came upon him—and in the doing of it. Repentance was a vital component implied in his four points:

1. Confess all known sin.
2. Search out all secret and doubtful things.

3. Confess the Lord Jesus openly.
4. Pledge your word that you will fully obey the Spirit.

As we will see in a later chapter, Evan had felt God's call to bring the youth in his own church together to pray for revival. This movement spread through western Wales, and small flashes of revival rain began to fall. Evan sent a letter to the groups and discussed his four points. The result was an intensification of the lightning.

"There is no doubt that the great awakening of the community took place between November 6th and 13th [1904]," wrote Brynmor Pierce Jones, a biographer of Evan Roberts. "It centered upon seven chapels in Loughor and Gorseinon." The outcome was such that Evan decided to put off his studies and, with the blessing of his teachers, began gathering more people into groups and praying for revival.[10]

David Howell and others in Wales at the beginning of the twentieth century lamented the relapse, rebellion, and refiner's fire that had befallen the principality. They knew that so much of the church in Wales had been trashed by rationalism in limpid pulpits and theologies that weakened confidence in the authority of the Bible. The results were seen in society. Though their voices were few—and though the youth who would cry out for repentance and revival was hidden in a dark coal mine—repentance would come and the lightning of revival would strike.

For that is the *tao*—the way—of the spiritual lightning we call revival.

CHAPTER 4

The *Tao* of Lightning

*His lightnings lit up the world; The
earth saw and trembled.*

—Psalm 97:4

Evan Roberts was like "a particle of radium" or "a consuming fire" that "cleared the channels of tears and sped the wheels of prayer throughout this district," said a church leader in Newcastle Emlyn.[1]

If that was the case, it was only because Evan himself had been struck by the lightning of God's revivifying energy.

The great end-times revival will be an interaction between heaven and earth just as lightning is an interaction between an energy-charged cloud and the ground beneath it. It will be the incursion of the transcendent into the immanent, just as a bolt of lightning is an invasion from above into the landscape below. It will also be the last incursion of God's *kairos* on the plane of *kronos* resulting in revival.

Propriety

When ancient observers contemplated natural phenomena, they began to see that all things have *propriety*, an appropriateness of being and an existential function unique to themselves. James Hannam points out that there was a constancy in natural phenomena that awoke inquiry about nature in the Middle Ages. Such constancy was the distinct propriety of natural phenomena.[2]

Propriety means there is a proper way for a thing to exist because it is the very nature of the thing itself. Chinese philosophers began speaking of the *tao*, that is, the way of a thing that made it what it was. *Tao* recognized the distinctive way of objects and phenomena as fitting into a larger pattern and giving them their meaning. All things together, therefore, existed as a unified whole in some great design. Thus the rightness of something that was its *tao* was discerned in the context of its relation to the grand scheme of creation. Harmony resulted from synchronization of the individual components of the natural world with the order of the cosmos itself. This was not only the music of the spheres but the *dance* of the spheres as well.

C. S. Lewis was fascinated by the *tao* principle in a biblical context and hence the larger connectedness it implied. For Lewis, *tao* expressed the objectivity of value: some things are objectively valid and others actually not true. Jesus thus spoke of His revelation as "the way and the truth and the life" (John 14:6 NIV). *Tao* is also found in Proverbs:

> There are three things which are too wonderful for me,
> Four which I do not understand:
> The *way* of an eagle in the sky,
> The *way* of a serpent on a rock,

The *way* of a ship in the middle of the sea,
And the *way* of a man with a maid. (30:18–19, italics added)

The *tao* of lightning teaches us—as we shall see in the next chapter—that first comes the energy-charged cloud, hovering above the ground. Turbulence roils inside the cloud, pressures intensify, and colliding forces build up to the point the lightning must be released. But there must be a zone of earth below to beckon and receive the bolt. The *tao* of lightning means the *kairos*, the opportune moment cannot come until the conditions in the cloud and those on earth are ready. Once this happens, the cloud's energy is shot to the prepared ground. The strike releases its electrical energy into the ground that has called it down.

SOVEREIGNTY

As we note elsewhere, there is a kind of sovereignty at work here: the cloud created the conditions by which the ground would call down the lightning at the precise point positioned to receive the bolt. The earth is significantly altered at that place of the bolt's strike. The bolt of revival lightning even changes the language of pit ponies!

Just as clouds are energized and empowered by physical forces, so, too, will the coming end-times revival be energized and empowered by spiritual forces—the presence of God in the cloud of His glory. The spiritual energy will whirl and intensify until the critical moment when the power will strike the earth at a prepared place and at a precise moment. The revival will be a dance between the sovereignty of God and human hearts. It will charge people, their institutions, and whole societies with energy that stimulates transformation. Lightning is frightening and dangerous, but it replenishes the weary and depleted, and so will the end-times revival lightning.

The spiritual, philosophical, and moral landscape of Wales as the twentieth century dawned was dissipated and exhausted. It had been plowed over, sown, and resown with many varieties of seed cultivated in Enlightenment rationalism, romantic idealism, and Roman hedonism. The Welsh also pulsed with Celtic mysticism and had supped on a smorgasbord of religions. The spiritual soil was drained of nutrients in the early twentieth century. It was starved for energy and life. It urgently needed revivification. *Wales needed to be struck by lightning.*

WALES IN NEED OF LIGHTNING

Wales in 1904 was in desperate need of the lightning of revival. David Horn, writing about conditions in Wales that led to the lightning, said that "the Christianizing of a nation had its own problems. Church-going people could easily become nominal, hiding spiritual decline behind ornate religiosity."[3]

No one could doubt the eloquence of the Welsh pulpit prior to the revival. The greatest preachers in that land spoke in a style called the *hwyl*. It was "professional and poetic" according to Horn. The problem was this oratorical splendor came "often at the expense of being spiritually nourishing to the hearer."

As I read the description of Welsh preaching at the outset of the twentieth century, juxtaposed with the laments of David Howell, I could not help but think of my old friend and associate at the Nixon White House, Charles Colson. Chuck was indicted and convicted of crimes related to the Watergate scandal and sent to prison in Alabama. A year before, as I described elsewhere, I had resigned my position at the White House and begun a journey that led me to the pastorate of a small church in south Alabama.

One day a friend called and told me of Chuck's new commitment to Christ. At first I was incredulous. Then the caller told me more and I became excited. He said Chuck's imprisonment was three hours from my home and asked if I would visit him. The warden gave me permission to come, and within a week I was en route from my home near Mobile to Montgomery and the federal prison at Maxwell Air Force Base.

Chuck and I were surprised when the warden allowed us to use his private conference room. As Chuck wrote in his spiritual biography, *Born Again*, we later discovered the reason we were given such an auspicious and private place for our meeting was that the room was bugged. Authorities hoped we would talk about the scandal that was about to bring down President Nixon, but all they received was two newfound brothers in Christ praying and talking about Chuck's family.

I asked Chuck how he thought the Watergate scandal happened, and I will never forget his response. "We didn't take time to reflect," he said. Actions have consequences, and there was a failure to seriously contemplate potential outcomes.

Then Chuck said something that broke my heart. He was well-known at the White House—and even by his critics—for his sharp analytical mind. That's why he could so readily conclude that the actions that produced the huge scandal were mindless. Now, though, as a serious follower of Jesus Christ, Chuck was applying those analytical skills to the state of American Christianity.

His question to me that afternoon was stark: If there are so many churches in America, why is there so little transformation?

Wales at the close of the nineteenth century and the opening of the twentieth had golden-throated preachers, glorious music, and beautiful churches, and yet there was a spiritual, philosophical, and moral dearth in the principality. So America—and much of Christendom above the equator—has glitzy religious celebrities, megachurches, and big institutions, yet the therapeutic pulpit of the twenty-first century has brought the focus away from the transcendent holiness of God and centered it on the immanent scale to the extent that the fear of God has left the land.

George Barna reported in 2017 that only "17 percent of Christians who consider their faith important and attend church regularly actually have a biblical worldview."[4]

Back to the Welsh pulpit in 1900–1904: the spiritual dearth amid entertaining and riveting rhetoric "only increased the longing for yet another national revival that might recalibrate and resurrect a more vital Christian experience, and a number of prayer initiatives were born throughout the land."[5]

A spiritual cloud was already hovering over the ground, and the charge was building that would summon the energy churning inside to hurl its bolt and revive the people, the churches, and the nation itself.

May God's presence in the cloud brood over us in these troubled times, and may we call down its lightning!

CHAPTER 5

The Hovering Cloud

*Then the cloud covered the tent of meeting, and
the glory of the Lord filled the tabernacle.*

—Exodus 40:34

At the very beginning of creation, everything was in a prenatal state—*tohu* (formlessness) and *bohu* (emptiness). "And the *Ruach Elohim* was hovering [brooding] upon the face of the waters," says the Hebrew Bible in Genesis 1:2.

The Ruach Elohim is the wind, the energy of God, that is, the Spirit of the Lord.

That great hovering presence nurtured the fetus of earth with the fullest quality of life. The Spirit brought *bios*, life capable of existing in the finite world that would be the dwelling place for God's image bearers: those who could receive, flourish in, and give back His love. But the Ruach Elohim also seeded *Zoe*, which is the infinite, eternal life quality of God Himself within the image bearer.

The image bearer for which this glorious cosmos was made would be able to smell the fruit of the earth's orchards, caress the face of a baby, embrace the image bearer who was other, and behold the lavish colors of paradise. At the same time the image bearer could commune with the Father in the realm that transcended the created world. And the transcendent Father who inhabits the highest heaven would walk in the garden of the immanent world of time, space, and matter.

Dimensions would overlap. Communion and relationship between heaven and earth, between *kairos* and *kronos*, between Creator and the created would be unobstructed. Zoe and bios were never to be separated in the Creator's intentional design. Their union would thus enable a wonderful interaction between heaven and earth that would make the created world a paradise where love would be the very atmosphere.

All of this because of the presence that hovered over His creation like a cloud and nurtured like a mother.

Love works only where there is freedom to reject it. Love is not a rapist; it does not force itself on another. It is offered and either received or rejected. There must be freedom to make the choice. God is free, and if His image bearers are truly to be like Him, they must be free as well. Therefore, God plants two trees in the garden of Eden and provides full disclosure to His image bearers: one is the Tree of Life and the other the Tree of Knowledge of Good and Evil, which promises the world but leads to separation, fragmentation, and death.

To eat the fruit of the latter is to lose the quality of Zoe, the rich blossom of the Tree of Life. It is to be reduced to bios only, that is, mere existence. In that state, love will be pared down and deconstructed in a tragic reductionism. Rather than selflessly pure *agape* love that is the very heart of God, the image bearers will pursue the love of self-interest. Without the agape nurtured by Ruach Elohim, love will mutate and become exploitation.

Tragically, it all happens. Adam and Eve, in whose flesh we all are encompassed, chomp into the forbidden fruit. Now come pain, thorn, and thistle.

And death.

CLOUD OF GOD'S PRESENCE

But the Father has not forgotten. While it is painful to His great heart to experience the rejection of His love by His image bearers who were created to receive and relish in it, He does not give up. He sends His life-giving, love-laden presence repeatedly, like a cloud hovering over all history.

This is called revival. The Ruach Elohim broods again over certain places, nurturing love and life. The Spirit of God refreshes the weary, restores the broken, renews the damaged and scarred, *revivifies* those whose souls are becoming as numb as death, guides the lost back to the home of God's own heart, for which, as Augustine said long ago, they were made. In revival, the Ruach Elohim recovers the strays, purifies the sin-stained, and beautifies those marred by evil's claws. Through revival, the Holy Spirit brings back the cosmos of civilizations that have fallen back into *tohubohu* as well as human lives languishing in the ruins of those toxic societies.

Chalaph is one of the Hebrew words associated with revival in the Old Testament. Among its meanings is the idea of changing, replacing, or moving something from one place to another. It also means to "come over," "hover over," or "dwell over." So the perspective given by using *chalaph* is that "revival occurs when God 'hovers' or 'dwells' over His people in order to alter or substitute the undesirable circumstances with God's desired circumstances."[1]

The *Shekinah*, the glory cloud hovering over the mercy seat of the ark of the covenant inside the temple's Holy of Holies, was the cloud of God's presence. There is the *objective* presence of God, that is, the promise of the presence always, whether we are aware of it or not. There is also the *subjective* presence, namely, the presence of the promise that is manifest to us in our minds, emotions, and even our senses—as we will explore in chapters to come.

The cloud brings the manifest presence. Some theologians now call it the theophanic cloud, meaning, the cloud of the Lord's appearing. So the Lord instructs Moses to warn his high priest brother, Aaron, that he must not enter the Holy of Holies inside the great veil casually or on his own schedule. If he does, he will die, because the glory of God is so intense that unprepared human biology cannot endure it. God says, "I will appear in the cloud over the mercy seat" (Lev. 16:2).

A time will come when Israel will inhabit the promised land. There they will build the temple that will replace the tabernacle, the mobile center of worship required in their wilderness wanderings. God would be manifest in the temple (as He had been in the tabernacle) in the cloud of His presence. His glory cloud would be so magnificent "that when the priests came from the holy place, the cloud filled the house of the LORD" with such intensity that they "could not stand to minister because of the cloud." It reminded Solomon, the temple's builder, that the Lord had promised "that He would dwell in the thick cloud" (1 Kings 8:10–12).

The promise had special meaning for the Hebrews, for they recalled that God had guided their fathers through the Sinai wilderness with the pillar of fire by night and the cloud by day. This had been a literal cloud, the union of the material and the spiritual.

There is here a foreshadowing of the Christ, in whom the physical and spiritual are perfectly merged. Thus the apostle Paul spoke of the continuing meaning of the cloud in the New Covenant era: "I do not want you to be unaware, brethren, that our fathers were all under the cloud and all passed through the sea; and all were baptized into Moses in the cloud and in the sea" (1 Cor. 10:1–2). All that happened to the Hebrews in the Exodus experience are examples for us, he says. That history was "written for our instruction, upon whom the ends of the ages have come" (v. 11). Thus the cloud that was physically manifest to the Hebrews during their passage through the sea and the wilderness has a continuing spiritual significance across time for those in the new covenant of grace.

The cloud of nature, charged with natural energy, is a type of the cloud of supernature, roaring with spiritual energy. The Hebrews of the Exodus were "baptized into Moses" in their passage through cloud and sea, but we are baptized into Christ as we enter the spiritual cloud that carries His powerful life.

Peter, James, and John experienced this when they climbed a certain "high mountain" with Jesus one day. There Jesus "was transfigured before them." That is, they saw Jesus as He really was, His essence as the divine Savior and Lord who has entered human time and history. They also saw Moses and Elijah talk with the Lord. Simon Peter blurted out that he would build "three tabernacles here, one for You, and one for Moses, and one for Elijah." But right in the middle of Peter's declaration, "a bright cloud overshadowed them, and behold, a voice out of the cloud said, 'This is My beloved Son, with whom I am well-pleased; listen to Him!'"

The three disciples immediately fell to the ground, "terrified." But Jesus "came to them and touched them and said, 'Get up, and do not be afraid.'" Peter, James, and John "lifting up their eyes . . . saw no one except Jesus Himself alone" (Matt. 17:1–8).

This is a description of authentic revivals of the past and the end-times revival—it is all about the Lord Jesus Christ. The spiritual cloud comes and hovers over a place, and its energy begins to impact individual men and women. The Lord is revealed to their hearts as He really is. Everything is stripped away until they see "Jesus Himself alone."

THE SPIRITUAL CLOUD OVER WALES

And so in late 1904 a spiritual cloud hovered over Loughor, a hamlet in Wales. The lightning simmering inside the cloud found ground there that beckoned to it to strike. What was so special about this place that the cloud—the presence—came and hovered there?

Unstable periods of history are preparatory stages for revival. Among the ways of God are these:

The Deeper the Darkness, the Brighter the Light
> The people who walk in darkness
> Will see a great light;
> Those who live in a dark land,
> The light will shine on them. (Isa. 9:2)

Darkness brings a hungering for light. Deep in a cavern, the light from the smallest match will appear as a torch. As societies grow darker, a sincere quest for light develops.

The Worse the Desolation, the Greater the Restoration
> Then I will make up to you for the years
> That the swarming locust has eaten,

> The creeping locust, the stripping locust and the gnawing
> locust, . . .
> You will have plenty to eat and be satisfied
> And praise the name of the LORD your God,
> Who has dwelt wondrously with you;
> Then My people will never be put to shame. (Joel 2:25–26)

This promise is for God's covenant people, a remnant amid the nations. In the New Covenant era, the heirs of the covenant constitute the authentic church. As the church is blessed, the nation shares the benefit. What happens in the church determines what happens in the nation.

The More Painful the Wound, the More Wonderful the Healing

> "I have heard of You by the hearing of the ear;
> But now my eye sees You;
> Therefore I retract,
> And I repent in dust and ashes." . . .

> The LORD restored the fortunes of Job when he prayed for his friends, and the LORD increased all that Job had twofold. . . . The LORD blessed the latter days of Job more than his beginning. (Job 42:5–6, 10, 12)

The More Dismal the Outlook, the Greater the Manifestation of Hope

> One of the criminals who were hanged there was hurling abuse at Him, saying, "Are You not the Christ? Save Yourself and us!" But the other answered, and rebuking him said, "Do you not even fear God, since you are under the same sentence of condemnation?

And we indeed are suffering justly, for we are receiving what we deserve for our deeds; but this man has done nothing wrong." And he was saying, "Jesus, remember me when You come in Your kingdom!" And He said to him, "Truly I say to you, today you shall be with Me in Paradise." (Luke 23:39–43)

The More Unstable the World, the Nearer the Approach of Revival

There will be signs in sun and moon and stars, and on the earth dismay among nations, in perplexity at the roaring of the sea and the waves, men fainting from fear and the expectation of the things which are coming upon the world; for the powers of the heavens will be shaken. Then they will see THE SON OF MAN COMING IN A CLOUD with power and great glory. But when these things begin to take place, straighten up and lift up your heads, because your redemption is drawing near. (Luke 21:25–28)

Jesus is speaking of His second coming and the end of the age, but He is also showing the principle that great instability precedes the interventions of God in human history, culminating in Christ's return.

All this is true because, said Jesus, those are "blessed" who "hunger and thirst for righteousness" (Matt. 5:6).

∽

In 1904, the cloud of God's presence brooded over the little village of Loughor. There dwelt young Evan Roberts, who, as we will see in a later chapter, became the tallest lightning rod for the bolt that would electrify Wales with a mighty revival.

Loughor and its people, including Evan and his family, had

learned the ways of God. The darkness of the coal mines where Evan, his father, and most of the men of Loughor worked certainly stirred a yearning for light. For some, like Evan, who took his Bible with him into the pits daily, their heart hunger would be for spiritual light as well as physical light.

The people of Loughor also knew desolation and the breakthroughs of the joy of restoration. They remembered strip-mined hillsides that were allowed to rest had later become covered with rich forests. Some grasped the deeper lesson: God would take lives and families that had been cruelly scoured and use that scraped surface to seed glorious fruit. Many knew the chill of the alarm that meant an explosion or collapse had occurred down in the pits, the terror of thinking of loved ones trapped down there, and the ache of bereavement.

Everyone knew the possibility of disaster because they knew the families of David Lewis, Morgan Saunders, Thomas White, John Talmin, and Thomas Bowen, all of whom had died in the Broadoak mine in 1897. Evan was a boy when that tragedy occurred, but by age twenty-six, he was working in the mines because his father had been injured and needed his son down there with him.

Those who had run to God in those ripping moments had ultimately found His joy and peace, even as anxiety tried to pool in their souls again with every sounding of the alarm.

On October 3, 1904, the people of Loughor and Glamorganshire did not know that the spiritual lightning bolt of revival would soon hit. They were consumed with a tragic railway accident that day. The Great Western London Express had left Llanelly fifteen minutes late and had added speed as quickly as possible. The train had two engines, and that dual power soon had the passenger-filled cars zipping on the track at fifty miles an hour (another report says the speed was twenty to twenty-five miles per hour).

Suddenly, a half mile from Loughor, the lead engine careened off the tracks, and after a hurling somersault came to rest in a marsh. The second engine also left the track, dragging four coaches with it. That engine plowed a one-hundred-yard gash through the muddy ground before it came to a halt. As it did, the four coaches telescoped into it.

"The roar of escaping steam, and the grinding and splintering of woodwork was nearly drowned by the heartrending cries of women and children, and savage shoutings of men for the moment bereft of senses and manhood," a newspaper correspondent reported.[2] Five people died, and ninety-four were injured.

Though Loughor had once been the site of a Roman station, and in 1904 still trailed "among its mines and tin-works some remainders of an ancient glory," it had become a backwater to which few in Wales gave any thought. The little town "was probably unknown beyond a few miles until it acquired unhappy fame" because of the railway accident, wrote H. Elvet Lewis.[3]

NATIONAL TRAIN WRECK

In 1902, David Howell feared his country was heading toward a train wreck spiritually, theologically, morally, and culturally. Like the Loughor train two years later, it seemed as if things were lunging off the track. Institutions essential to civil order and the well-being of the people were being upended. It was as if the 1904 tragedy were a parable signifying the chaos toward which Wales and its people were speeding.

The principality, Howell believed, was becoming increasingly unstable as it seemed to forget previous outpourings of revival. "Family worship is disappearing," he wrote in a late 1902 open letter.

Sunday school, once so vibrant in Wales and vital for teaching children and teens about biblical foundations, "is only just holding its own," Howell continued. "Congregations in many places are lessening," with the keeping of the Sabbath "a matter of debate." The prayer meeting so much at the heart of Wales's church life "is nearly extinct," he lamented. "The authority of the Bible and the foundational truths of Christianity are being judged in the court of reason and criticism." At the same time, "unshakeable belief in the unseen, the miraculous and the supernatural is questioned openly." The outcomes were everywhere evident, including "the curse of drink raising its head in town and countryside. . . . The desire for pleasure has totally captivated the age." A national train wreck seemed inevitable. Howell had every reason to wonder what went wrong.

David Matthews, who would become a friend of Evan Roberts and personally experience the power of the moving of God, also had cause to question what had happened to his country. Wales had known revival almost every decade, Matthews recalled. It was known as "The Land of Revivals" and "The Land of Song." Matthews remembered the spiritual giants who had nurtured the principality: Vavassor Powell, Griffiths Jones, William Williams, Howell Harris, Christmas Evans, and Richard Owen.[4]

Despite all this, violence was spreading across the land and superstition was taking root. J. Vynrwy Morgan, another church leader during the revival, would sometimes be a critic of Evan Roberts and the movement, though he stressed he meant "no hostility" in his critique. Nevertheless, he, too, was concerned for his society and the world. In the decade that ended with 1901, "Mohammedism added five million to its membership in India" while "our evangelical churches have to report arrested progress."[5]

Morgan was concerned for the state of the Welsh youth because "a new world has been opened up for them." In this new age, these young people were "being laughed out of their religious scruples and home-made modesty." There were even influential voices in the Welsh culture that were warning the young "against the cultivation of moral dreams and the pursuit of spiritual shadows," telling them that "nothing is sacred . . . but what is sanctioned by reason." Because of this, young people "brought up in an atmosphere of reverence" were "found sitting in the seat of the scornful."[6]

Then came the cloud.

There are many movements that people call revival that do not necessarily constitute a true move of God because they are human-centered rather than God-centered. The focus is more on the blessing than the painful, transformative work of God in a person that brings glory to God. "He [or she] who has suffered in the flesh has ceased from sin" (1 Peter 4:1). True revival is energizing and inspiring, but it is also searing and surgical. This is why we must come to situations in which we are desperate for righteousness. Short of that, we fail to understand the importance of the recognition and confession of sin and a passionate desire to repent. We mistake counterfeit spirituality for true revival and miss the genuine work of God in our midst.

CHAPTER 6

The Ground Below

[Revival] presupposes a declension.
—CHARLES FINNEY[1]

*Before every revival in history, deteriorating
conditions have been evident in secular
society and among God's people.*
—MALCOM McDOW[2]

Michael McQuilken was full of anticipation on August 20, 1975, as he climbed toward the domed summit of California's Moro Rock. The massive granite formation towered almost seven thousand feet over Sequoia National Park and the spectacular canyon gouged out far below by the Kaweah River. Michael was accompanied by his brothers Sean and Jeff, his sister Mary, and her friend Margie. The teenagers knew the view from the crest of the Great Western Divide would be breathtaking.

But not long after reaching the top, the youths noted some strange phenomena. For one thing, their hair was standing straight up, as if an invisible hand were pulling on it. They laughed at each other. This was before cell phones and selfies, but Mary had an Instamatic camera, and they had fun taking photos of one another and their standing-on-end hair.

Michael hoisted his right arm. He later said, "The ring I had on began to buzz so loudly that everyone could hear it."

The summit became colder and hail began to thrash the rock, so the group decided to head down. They had gone just a short distance when a massive bolt of lightning zeroed in on them. Michael was in the vortex of "the brightest light I have ever seen." He compared it to an intense burst of searing light like that of an arc welding device. His brain reacted. He felt time grinding to a slow drag. Gravity itself seemed to be whisked away. He had a sensation of weightlessness. In the midst of it all, Michael was pounded with a "deafening explosion."

His head cleared and he was aware that his brother Sean had crumbled to his knees. Michael saw smoke surging from Sean's back. Sean had drawn the direct hit of the bolt, and Michael rushed to his side. "He was still alive," he recounted. "I put out the embers on his back and elbows and carried him down the path toward the parking lot, with the rest of the group following."

On the way down, they passed a woman frantically trying to help her husband, whose chest was burned just over his heart. Michael found out later the man died.[3]

Michael McQuilken and all the people who went through the experience that day on Moro Rock learned a powerful lesson: before lightning strikes, changes come on the ground below, and those phenomena actually attract the bolt.

If the ground on which one stands is suddenly charged with energy, it's time to get ready for the strike.

In the cloud above, a strong electrical field begins to seethe with a negative charge. Meanwhile, the ground below reacts through the buildup of a positive charge. The result is that "an intense reaction builds between the cloud and the ground." The bolt is "the runaway force that discharges this field."[4]

Without the changes in the ground below, the electrically charged cloud energy stays in the sky. Cloud-to-earth lightning requires the crisis of the buildup of the charge on the ground. As the McQuilken band of hikers discovered that August day in 1975, the terrain under the cloud experiences a crisis that is part of the buildup of the positive charge that draws the lightning to a particular place.

The Spiritual Principle

The spiritual lesson in this natural phenomenon is that crisis in the ground we inhabit is what prompts us to cry out to God for revival.

Christian philosopher Romano Guardini, writing in 1956, believed the world of his future—our contemporary world—would be full of intense crises. In the modern period people would forget God and His revelation of Himself, but in the postmodern era (some say we live in the post-postmodern age) individuals would sense something was missing.

"As the benefits of Revelation disappear ever more from the coming world, man will truly learn what it means to be cut off from Revelation," Guardini wrote. "As unbelievers deny Revelation more decisively, as they put their denial into more consistent practice, it will become the more evident what it really means to be a Christian."[5] (Guardini uses the word *revelation* to refer to God's disclosure of Himself to humanity.)

We think of crisis strictly in negative terms, but the Greek word *krisis* (from which we get the word *crisis*) actually has a positive edge. It speaks of "sundering" and "separation" but also a critical turning point that can be positive, as in the point at which healing overtakes a disease. *Krisis* is the arrival of a strategic point of decision when a person can turn away from an old course or lifestyle.[6]

The prophet Isaiah wrote:

> The people who walk in darkness
> Will see a great light;
> Those who live in a dark land,
> The light will shine on them. (9:2)

His point was that the deeper the darkness, the brighter and more precious the light until we come to yearn for it.

Surely, through the Holy Spirit, Isaiah was prophesying the coming of the Messiah into the dark world via a tiny nation that did indeed "walk in darkness," into a world itself plunged into the great, grim abyss of evil through humanity's fall into sin. Specifically, there was a bleak Friday afternoon when Jesus died to lift all humankind and creation out of darkness. From noon to about 3:00 p.m. that day, it seemed that night had come (Matt. 27:45; Mark 15:33; Luke 23:44–45). But the deep darkness was overwhelmed on the third day by the glorious light of Christ's resurrection. Jesus' followers had been swallowed up in the darkness of Friday afternoon, but they glowed in the brilliance of Sunday morning!

Amazement over the Pacific

Many years ago, during a long flight from Tokyo to Los Angeles, I experienced a living illustration of the meaning of this passage, and it has been special to me ever since. A few hours after our 9:00 p.m. departure from Tokyo, we had had a meal and many hunkered under blankets to try to sleep. Flight attendants pulled the shades though there was no light in the sky outside that could have seeped into the cabin. There was no turbulence, so there was no sense of the speeding jet's movement. It was as if we were suspended in a primordial nothingness.

I sat by a window and occasionally lifted the shade to see if I could see anything outside. Everything was black: the cloudless night outside the fuselage and the heaving, deep, dark Pacific below. I fought claustrophobia and slept fitfully.

After what seemed hours and for what could have been the hundredth time, I lifted the shade again. What I saw caused me to gasp. Far out on the eastern horizon I could see a shard of brilliant red-orange light splitting the two crucibles of darkness, the sky and the sea. I had forgotten how beautiful a sunrise was until I saw it against the backdrop of the deep night.

I wanted to run up and down the aisles, rip the blindfolds off sleeping eyes, throw up all the shades, and shout, "Arise! Shine! Your light has come!"

I didn't, of course.

I remained in my seat and watched the brilliant light overwhelm the crisis of being enveloped in darkness above, below, and everywhere. I saw a living demonstration that night of the lessons we've touched on already:

- The deeper the darkness the brighter the light.
- Darkness is troubling, but the light is blessed calm and peace.
- In the Lord Jesus Christ, the light overcomes the darkness (John 1:5).

Eifion Evans, a historian of the 1904 Welsh Revival, understood well the sequence of crisis and revival and wrote an essay titled "Darkness Before the Dawn." He noted:

> The revivals of the sixteenth and eighteenth centuries came to an apostate, declining, expiring Church, while those of the seventeenth and nineteenth centuries took place against the backdrop of a dormant, listless, and unconcerned Church. . . . The resultant systems of deism, rationalism and moralism had crippled the Church [in the eighteenth century], reducing its effectiveness and bringing about a drastic degeneration in spiritual life.[7]

THE RIDDLE OF DARKNESS

What, then, is the riddle of the darkness? Why does God apparently allow us to fall into such crises that even King David asks, "Where are you?" Why does God permit human depravity to sweep its bitter scythe over the face of the world? Why does He permit evil to seem to win the day?

The psalmist fretted over such things. But the answer again is always *the deeper the darkness, the brighter the light.* Further, the deeper the darkness, the more we come to crave the light. And that leads us to the place of passionate heart prayer for God to send the lightning of revival.

Why must we be brought to the point that we must ask?

Earlier, we noted Romano Guardini's observation: "As the benefits of Revelation disappear even more from the coming world, man will truly learn what it means to be cut off from Revelation."[8] This brings crisis. The remnant begins to hunger and thirst for righteousness. This agony of soul leads to the intercession that calls down revival lightning, which was God's desire all along.

It is God's intentional, sovereign will to bring the lightning of revival, but He has set boundaries for Himself at the borders of our freedom. This is part of what it means for us to be made in the image of God and to be truly human. Maybe life would have been simpler if there had been no serpent and only one tree in the garden, but we would have no freedom and nothing to choose.

Stephen Olford called revival "that strange and sovereign work of God in which He visits His own people, restoring, reanimating, and releasing them into the fullness of His blessing."[9] Thus Evan Roberts would "remind people that revival was God's achievement alone" and that men and women "are only the instruments."[10]

CUT OFF FROM GOD'S REVELATION

The Welsh Revival of 1904 and all other moves of God in human history show that, in the midst of a spiritual crisis, the Holy Spirit takes the initiative in preparing the ground for revival. The Spirit of God is the wind that blows where it will (John 3:8), and Spirit-indwelt people are impacted by it. As they are energized, they minister revival across the land. So it will be in the end.

What then was the crisis at the end of the nineteenth century that necessitated this divine intervention in Wales? It was the onslaughts of powerful nineteenth-century movements like higher criticism (which denied the Bible was the inspired Word of God), Darwinism (which attributed creation to random forces rather than intelligent design), the now-discredited psychoanalytic theories of Sigmund Freud, and the emergence of Karl Marx's economic theory. But hardly any philosophical system was as toxic as the rationalism that had sprung from the turmoil of eighteenth-century Europe.

In his poem "Dover Beach," nineteenth-century British essayist Matthew Arnold described the ebb tide of religion in his time:

> The Sea of Faith
> Was once, too, at the full, and round earth's shore
> Lay like the folds of a bright girdle furled;
> But now I only hear
> Its melancholy, long, withdrawing roar.[11]

DAVID HOWELL'S CONCERN

In Cardiff, David Howell became increasingly alarmed. Born in 1831, by 1902 Howell was a veteran spiritual warrior. He knew "judgment must begin at the house of God" (1 Peter 4:17 KJV). If there were problems in the culture, the search for the cause should not begin in the spheres of education, government, media, and the arts—though these could contribute to the health or sickness of society—but at the church and its theology. Christopher Dawson wrote:

> Christianity is the soul of Western civilization, and when the soul is gone the body putrefies. What is at stake is not the external profession of Christianity, but the inner bond which holds society together, which links man to man and the order of the state to the order of nature. And when this has gone nothing remains but the principle of brute force which is essentially unreconcilable with a pluralist society.[12]

The church is to be the salt that preserves the heritage that forms a nation's very soul. It is to be the light-giver that guides people in a society to walk in the truth that is life itself.

Every nation, said Harvard political scientist Samuel Huntington—along with Dawson, T. S. Eliot, C. S. Lewis, and many others—is built on a seminal worldview that addresses life's ultimate questions. The church is therefore at the headwaters, preserving and propagating an essential belief system on which whole civilizations rest. If it goes bad, everything downstream will become toxic.

Howell's understanding of Wales's challenges and the hope for all nations had been sharpened through decades of ministry. He had experienced the powerful move of God in 1859 in Wales and Britain. He would cap his career as dean of St. David's Cathedral in Cardiff and die in late 1903—but not before penning a letter that would stir the passion for revival. The aching in his heart moved others to prayer, and initial waves of revival began to impact Howell's region, Cardiganshire, in early 1904. From there the cloud expanded, reaching Glamorganshire, the home of Evan Roberts, by the autumn of 1904. The impact of Howell and the open letter he wrote, which was widely published, was such that Jesse Penn-Lewis called him "the prophet of the revival."[13]

As the godly aged pastor wrote, Howell began with a warning about the state of the church in Wales. In fact, his concern in 1902 might describe the conditions we face in our society that should prompt a cry for God to move among us in true revival. He wrote:

> The preaching, it is said, is able, scholarly, interesting and instructive; it is however accompanied with but little unction and anointing—there is no smiting of the conscience, no laying bare the condition of the soul as in times past. The terminology of

former ages, such as conviction, conversion, repentance, adoption, mortification of sin, self-loathing, and such like, has become to a great extent foreign and meaningless. . . . The authority of the Bible and the fundamental truths of Christianity are being weighed in the balance of reason and criticism, as though they were nothing more than human opinions. A steadfast faith in the invisible, the miraculous, and the supernatural is regarded as open to question. . . . But what of the remedy? . . . A Holy Spirit religion is the only cure for the moral and spiritual disease of Wales at this time. . . . Take note: if it were known that this was my last message to my fellow-countrymen throughout the length and breadth of Wales, before being summoned to judgement, the light of eternity already breaking over me, it would be, that the principal need of my country and my dear nation at present is still spiritual revival through a special outpouring of the Holy Spirit.[14]

Anyone in the late nineteenth century who doubted Howell's painful assessment needed to look no farther than Bala Theological College, a flagship institution, and its principal, Lewis Edwards. In his time, Edwards was an intellectual twin to some scholars today who seek to adjust the biblical texts to the philosophical and theological currents of the age. Eifion Evans, however, recognized that Edwards was trying to defend the Scriptures from the rationalistic assault, but he turned to the tools of rationalism to do so. In Evans's view, Edwards was "using the weapons of the flesh to defend the citadel of the Spirit."[15]

The great threat of rationalism to the church was to the conviction of truth. Rather than a confident "thus saith the Lord" ringing from pulpits impacted by the age of rationalism, there was an irresolute, ambivalent "this may be the word of God . . . but who can be sure?" The scholarly, interesting, instructive eloquence that was propounded through many pulpits was a substitute for the Word of God, which is "living and active and sharper than any two-edged sword" (Heb. 4:12).

Negative Effect

Thus all this spiritual-psychological-institutional frothing in Wales in the years preceding the revival had a negative effect on the culture at large. And since the health of the nation is directly linked to the health of the church, toxicity in the churches—whether in belief or practice—sickens and poisons everything: family, education, civil governance, business and the marketplace, media, and the arts. When the church goes bad, the character of the nation suffers. Such a condition calls for the salt of God's Word, but confidence in the power of the Bible was undermined by rationalism, psychologism, and the trendy philosophies of the day.

In 1897, Calvinist Methodist leader Josiah Thomas lamented the skepticism and atheism of his age.

"Our age is an age of doubt," wrote Welshman Garmon Roberts, in 1901.[16]

D. M. Phillips described the period prior to the revival of 1904 as characterized by "uncertainty" caused by the influence of agnosticism, which had "spread like a hoarfrost over the life of the most faithful religious people in our churches."[17]

The character of a nation or society is determined by the character of the people and their institutions. W. S. Sangster provided insight into how the effects of sickened churches that stood at the spiritual and moral headwaters of the culture poisoned the whole and how the revival healed the waters of the church and then society itself. "When the Welsh Revival broke out in 1904, some people dismissed it as a wave of emotional fanaticism," Sangster wrote in 1957. Ultimately, however, they changed their minds . . . because they heard, wherever the revival went, that people were paying old and neglected, and half-forgotten debts. A commercial traveler told me once of the scorn with which he and other business men heard the early reports of the revival. But, when it began to pay debts that they had written off as hopeless, they looked upon it as a miracle and they criticized it no more. . . . A *lifting of common morality* is an early and inevitable consequence of re-born religion.[18]

Seasons of revival rise up repeatedly "from the presence of the Lord" and "emerge in the providence of God at a time of crisis," wrote revival scholar Eifion Evans. He continued:

When true religion is at a premium, when the Word of God is scarce and the lamp of God burns low in the land, then it is that the irresistible energies of the Holy Spirit burst forth with a vigour seldom witnessed more than once in any one generation. In the midst of the spiritual deadness there has always been a faithful remnant who had wisdom to discern and compassion to mourn the languishing state.[19]

What is the charge in the ground below that calls down lightning? It is the prayers of the saints, prompted by crisis. So Pierce Jones wrote that the "last six months before the Awakening in November 1904, were marked by almost desperate seeking after the blessing."[20] This intense intercession arose from the remnant to which Evans referred. It was set apart for God and His purposes in the world. Those who comprise the remnant are the lightning rods by which whole societies can experience the blessings of revival.

CHAPTER 7

The Church and Revival

The manifold wisdom of God might now be
made known through the church to the rulers
and the authorities in the heavenly places.

—EPHESIANS 3:10

T he authentic church is the most potent entity in the world.

The major difference between the holders of temporal rule and the church is that governing institutions may legislate and force change, but the Spirit-indwelt church ministers transformation. Change is often cosmetic, thus external, and cyclical, but transformation is inside-out and enduring. Temporal powers have only the finite world from which to draw their strength, but the true church brings the might of heaven itself into the earth.

The Welsh Revival of 1904 proved that the genuine church of the Lord Jesus Christ is the most powerful entity in the world. The Welsh church in its many forms was the place where the lightning of revival struck and from whence it spread into the land. No other institution of society—including civil government, education, social reform agencies, the legal system, charities—could produce the transformation. It was a transformation, not just of individuals but of whole groups, like coal miners and athletes, which occurred through the revival that began in small gatherings in often obscure churches.

THE AUTHORITY OF THE KEYS

One day Jesus asked the disciples what people were saying about Him.

> "Some say John the Baptist; and others, Elijah; but still others, Jeremiah, or one of the prophets." He said to them, "But who do you say that I am?" Simon Peter answered, "You are the Christ, the Son of the living God." And Jesus said to him, "Blessed are you, Simon Barjona, because flesh and blood did not reveal this to you, but My Father who is in heaven. I also say to you that you are Peter, and upon this rock I will build My church; and the gates of Hades will not overpower it. I will give you the keys of the kingdom of heaven." (Matt. 16:13–19)

Simon Peter's acknowledgment of Jesus as the Christ, the Anointed One, the Messiah, is the fundamental confession of the church. The keys symbolize the authority of the kingdom of God. It is given to the confessional community, the real church that joins in Peter's declaration of Jesus' identity. That church has many denominational designations and variances in doctrine, but all who hold to the essential doctrines expressed in the *kerygma*, the core message of the apostles, and make the fundamental confession of Christ constitute the body of Christ.

Kingdom authority was not given to the White House, the US Congress, the many parliaments, the Kremlin, or any other earthly power. The authentic church is the agency of God's authority in the world. This is not earthly power that depends on the strength of human flesh and muscle. Rather it is authority in and from the heavenlies, against the spiritual forces out to destroy the world (Eph. 3:1–10; 6:12).

Revival in a nation may ultimately impact governmental institutions, yet it does not begin there but in the church. Sometimes—as in first-century Rome and the former Soviet Union after the collapse of communism—the church that has the greatest impact has been previously driven underground, persecuted, and seemingly reduced to naught. But tyrants do not know that "God has chosen, the things that are not, so that He may nullify the things that are, so that no man may boast before God" (1 Cor. 1:28–29).

Rationalists in nineteenth-century Europe, including those in Britain and Wales, were certain the church was finished. Charles Darwin provided theories that seemed to rule out any need for a creator God, and the industrial revolution was proving what man could do to sustain and advance civilization. Rationalists wrote off the voices in the pulpit that warned of judgment and gave the good news of redemption as the pitiful remnants of a past superstitious age.

But none of those great powers could lift up sin-buried human beings, restore dignity to drunkards, bring joy and prosperity back into homes, cause judges to sit white-gloved in boredom, change the language of coal miners who had known only jargon that was like the filth in which they worked, cause the football teams that created frenetic fans to delay and even cancel games, turn out the lights at pubs on Saturday nights, and cause the cancellation of political rallies.

THE HOUSE OF REPRESENTATIVES

Crisis creates the hunger that compels the remnant to call down the lightning of true revival. As the representatives before the throne of the God of the nations in which they dwell, they invite Him to step in and intervene in their histories, cultures, societies, and civilization. This is the desire of God's heart, but He has established boundaries for His omnipotent power at the borders of our freedom. He will not step in until His designated representatives invite Him.

This is no illogical and inscrutable mode of relationship. We see it every day in the workings of representative government.[1] It is the idea behind the classic passage on intercession:

> [If] My people who are called by My name humble themselves and pray and seek My face and turn from their wicked ways, then I will hear from heaven, will forgive their sin and will heal their land. Now My eyes will be open and My ears attentive to the prayer offered in this place. For now I have chosen and consecrated this house that My name may be there forever, and My eyes and My heart will be there perpetually. (2 Chron. 7:14–16)

There are vital truths here we must understand if we are to be effective in praying on behalf of ourselves and our nation. The Welsh church leading up to and during the revival intuitively understood this and called down the lightning of spiritual awakening on their land. Here are some of the vital concepts:

- Those authorized to come before God for the earthly nation they inhabit are His people, called by His name. There is a remnant within every nation that walks in personal and intimate relationship with God. They bear His name within society. Old Testament Israel was God's possession. The genuine church in our time, made up of Jews and Gentiles alike, constitutes in our age "My people who are called by My name."

- A remnant people repent of their own sin as well as that of the nations where they reside, God hears and sees the repentance of the remnant as the repentance of the whole society and forgives and heals their land.

- God consecrated, or set apart, the temple as the place of His focus, looking for repentance and prayer. The New Testament shows that the authentic church is the invisible temple in the world today. But it is not invisible to God because He continues to have His eyes open and ears attentive to the intercessions made in the eternal temple—the body of Christ. God elects the church to represent Him before humanity and humanity to Him (1 Peter 2:9–10).

This does not mean that the church becomes a mighty political and military institution that sets up rulers over the people or a rich commodity whose accoutrements can be bought and sold by rich overlords. Such a thing calling itself "church" is not church at all.

In fact, in the kingdom of God there is an inverse relationship between bigness and smallness. In the kingdom economy, it is that which society thinks small in the sense of inconsequential that may be big in its eternal impact. On the other hand, that considered by the culture as big and mightily significant because of earthly, material stature is small in God's eyes.

When Jesus' disciples rebuked people for bringing their children for Him to touch, the Lord surprised them by telling them not to hinder the parents and their little ones, "for the kingdom of God belongs to such as these." Further, said Jesus, "Whoever does not receive the kingdom of God like a child will not enter it at all" (Mark 10:14–15).

No Little People or Places

Thus, as Frances Schaeffer wrote, and the Welsh Revival demonstrated, there are, in God's kingdom enterprise, "no little people and no little places."[2] In a coming chapter we will discuss the principle of "no little people," but as we think about the churches that were so vital in Wales in 1904, we will focus here on "no little *places.*"

Schaeffer is not speaking of physical bigness or material largeness of wealth. I have served much of my ministry in megachurches. At this writing I am a teaching pastor at Houston's Second Baptist Church, which has some eighty thousand members. Yet I have seen God work powerfully through this huge church. I have also served small churches in physical size that were huge in their impact for the kingdom.

Thus, when the lightning of revival began to hit Wales in 1904, it did not strike first upon and through magnificent cathedrals or the noble institutions of learning but in tiny chapels in the Welsh backwaters. The first news of the revival broke on November 10, 1904, in a report in the *Western Mail* newspaper, whose headlines heralded:

A Wonderful Preacher
Great Crowds of People Drawn to Loughor
Congregation Stay Till Half Past Two in the Morning

The ensuing article reported:

A remarkable religious revival is now taking place at Loughor. For some days a young man named Evan Roberts, a native of Loughor, but at present a student at Newcastle-Emlyn, has been causing great surprise by his extraordinary orations at Moriah Chapel, that place of worship having been besieged by dense crowds of people unable to obtain admission. Such excitement has prevailed that the road in which the chapel is situated has been lined with people from end to end.[3]

The newspaper was so intrigued by what was going on in Loughor that it sent a reporter to provide on-the-scene coverage. That such an extraordinary event would be happening at such a routine place was newsworthy. When most Welsh thought of Loughor at all, they probably recalled the deadly train wreck of a few weeks past.

The revival lightning would soon strike another seemingly insignificant locale. Eifion Evans described how the move of God came in Blaenannerch, "a small struggling village." It was, he wrote, "thoroughly Welsh and quietly unpretentious." Yet it was in that backwater that God chose to manifest His presence so powerfully that Evans noted Blaenannerch's "claim to fame is based exclusively on the remarkable scenes witnessed there in the autumn of 1904."[4]

THE THREAT OF RATIONALISM

But why Blaenannerch? Why Loughor? Why, indeed, the little slice of the United Kingdom called Wales? Perhaps the Holy Spirit found there a smallness of fleshly reliance and a bigness of dependence on the Spirit of God. Nevertheless, some of the Welsh churches at the outset of the twentieth century were embracing a bigness of rationalism and a smallness of regard for the authority of the Bible. In many ways they were failing their people, as Dean David Howell lamented at the start of the twentieth century.

In the opening decades of the twenty-first century, important facets of the American church are failing their people as well. There is a constant lament about the spiritual, moral, social, cultural, and political state of the nation. But as noted above, the Bible says judgment must begin at the house of the Lord. The state of the nation reflects the state of the core institution within the nation—the church.

There are many ministries, especially among evangelicals, seeking to impact the political sphere in the hope of turning around a wayward culture. I do not suggest that the evangelical church give up its efforts to bring spiritual renewal to the political sphere and help the nation find its way back to its Judeo-Christian biblical heritage, but there must be an even greater exertion of energy to understand and restore the church to its broader kingdom mission.

CHIEF DANGERS

At the dawn of the twentieth century, William Booth was asked what he thought the greatest dangers might be for the century ahead. He said:

> I consider that the chief dangers which confront the coming century will be religion without the Holy Ghost, Christianity without Christ, forgiveness without repentance, salvation without regeneration, politics without God, and heaven without hell.[5]

Both charismatics and evangelicals have trivialized the gospel of the kingdom by ignoring it or enculturating it. Some pentecostals and charismatics have reduced the gospel of the kingdom to the gospel of the spa, with an emphasis on health and wealth as the core of the message of Jesus and the Bible.

Some young evangelicals, in a fury to be relevant, have also abandoned the gospel of the kingdom and embraced the message of the emergent culture. They have rightly adopted new styles of communication to get the gospel across, but they have made the mistake of allowing style to drive theology. This has produced the same outcome of late nineteenth- and early twentieth-century rationalism; they have trimmed and coiffed sermonizing that has difficulty proclaiming, "Thus saith the Lord. . . ."

Christopher Smith and Melinda Lundquist Denton explored a major belief system of emergent culture youths in the twenty-first century, which they labeled "moralistic therapeutic deism." After interviewing some three thousand teens, the tenets of the religion were identified as:

- A god exists who created and ordered the world and watches over human life on earth.
- God wants people to be good, nice, and fair to each other, as taught in the Bible and by most world religions.
- The central goal of life is to be happy and to feel good about oneself.
- God does not need to be particularly involved in one's life except when God is needed to resolve a problem.
- Good people go to heaven when they die.

But all is not lost and what happened in Wales in the early twentieth century shows what can—and I believe will happen now—in the twenty-first. This is why it is important to study the Welsh Revival of 1904. We must gain hope and be prepared for the lightning. Despite the problems of theology and ecclesiology in the Welsh church, God sent His glory cloud over the land. The churches clinging to the crags surrounding mining villages, buried in backwater hamlets, and hanging on for dear life in struggling towns became strike zones of the mighty bolts of revival.

That's because, despite it all, they began to be filled with men and women who were the rods that called down the lightning.

CHAPTER 8

Evan Roberts and the Living Energy

Revivals have leaders. Sometimes one,
sometimes two. These leaders tend to be the
incarnation of the movement; they personify
the awakening in its most intense form.

—LEWIS A. DRUMMOND[1]

Evan Roberts was not the leader of the Welsh Revival. It did not begin with him or end with him. He was one of those men whom God chose to anoint in a singular and extraordinary way. That list of the great would include many spiritual giants, but as Richard Owen Roberts wrote of Roberts in 1989, "There are few men in all the annals of revival history who made such a profound impression in so brief a period."[2]

Thus by God's sovereign choice and promotion (Ps. 75:6–7), Evan became the tallest of the lightning rods that drew the 1904 revival bolt. God's eyes search the earth looking for those He can strengthen, whose heart is completely His (2 Chron. 16:9). What did God see in Evan Roberts? We cannot presume to answer such a question, but there are clues. Selwyn Hughes, in Pierce Jones's biography of Evan Roberts, lists characteristics that seem historically to constitute the profile of those God uses to initiate a revival:[3]

- Deep earnestness
- A desperate desire to see God work most powerfully
- Great faith
- Great patience
- A willingness to expend energy and labor fearlessly
- Determination
- Deep spirituality
- Fervency in prayer

Jones believed Evan Roberts to have all these characteristics, and so did Selwyn Hughes.

But Evan Roberts was also a mortal human, acutely aware of pride that he feared was hiding behind false humility and feigned meekness. This temptation to the "pride of life" (1 John 2:16) rose up even in prayer, and Evan once surprised some associates by borrowing a quote from John Henry Newman: "Pride ruled my will."[4]

Some of Evan's actions seemed inexplicable at times and even offensive. Anglican minister J. Vynrwy Morgan was one of those who zeroed in on Evan's flaws:

Evan Roberts was not intellectual in the sense intellectuality is commonly understood. He was moved more by his emotions than his ideas; and such ideas as he uttered had been current in the pulpit for generations. He was more intuitive that inductive or deductive. The broken sentences had more of the heat of passion than the dry light of truth. He had no fundamental doctrine, no system of theology, no distinctive ideal.[5]

CRITICISMS

Morgan wrote in 1906, after the revival. But Evan had to listen to caustic as well as positive criticisms throughout the days of his prominence as the perceived revival leader. He was highly sensitive, and the words sometimes sliced at his soul like a dagger. Evan felt himself "inferior when men with high degrees or high reputation were present," wrote Jones. Evan was especially aware that he had just six weeks of schooling preparing him for a college experience he never pursued. He knew, too, that his public-speaking skills were not the equal of men whose oratory had been honed over decades.[6]

Morgan, however, and other critics overlooked the fact that Evan was a perfect example of the principle discussed in the previous chapter: God uses "the things that are not, so that He may nullify the things that are" (1 Cor. 1:28). A one-paragraph summation of Evan's life in the *Western Mail* when he died in January 1951 provided a more balanced insight into the way most people not caught up in theological musings remembered Evan:

> He was a man who had experienced strange things. In his youth he had seemed to hold the nation in the palm of his hands. He endured strains and underwent great changes of opinion and outlook, but his religious convictions remained firm to the end.[7]

No doubt some of the criticisms aimed at Evan were couched in the subtleties of the conformist-nonconformist tensions prevalent in Wales and other parts of Great Britain at the time. The non-conformity movement consisted of those churches that did not align with the Church of England. Welsh nonconformists included Congregationalists, Baptists, Quakers, Calvinistic Methodists, and Wesleyan Methodists. Evan was a Calvinist Methodist, and many revival gatherings—though not all—were centered on Calvinistic Methodist churches (often referred to as chapels) rather than the great cathedrals and centers of the established church.

There were two strands of nonconformity that complicated the situation: the Reformed, whose origins were in John Calvin, and the revivalist-charismatic, stemming from eighteenth-century awakenings and the great revival of 1859. "The meshing of the two created the particular character of Welsh Nonconformity," said historian R. Tudur Jones.[8] The Calvinist strand stressed obedience to the written Word, while the revivalist-charismatic component centered on the necessity of the Holy Spirit's anointing.

Many seminary-trained, theologically sophisticated, experienced pastors and other church leaders have been caught in the stormy seas between these two positions. Think of Cape Horn at the southern tip of South America, where the Atlantic and Pacific collide in mighty tempests. Evan Roberts, untrained and inexperienced, sometimes found himself in these heaving crosscurrents, and some of his mistakes were made while trying to negotiate the turbulent waters of doctrine and style.

Bridge Between Factions

At the same time, Evan and the revival movement constituted a bridge between traditionalist and charismatic factions. As R. Tudur Jones pointed out—and we will see in more detail in later chapters—when the Calvinist and revivalist-charismatic strands "were balanced, church life combined strength of doctrine and warmth of experience, organizational stability and dynamic spirituality." Yet as Evan and many church leaders since have learned—and to which I can attest—it is "difficult to maintain this equilibrium."[9]

Evan Roberts was a human being with the weaknesses and frailties shared by all men and women. As is the case with almost anyone who rises to a measure of fame, sometimes Evan's errors became public. But such incidents remind us that God uses humans who make themselves available to Him, perfect and extraordinary in giftedness and finesse or not. After all, we are not to be in wonder of the lightning rod but awed by the lightning and, above all, its giver.

The charge in the ground of Evan's life that summoned the living energy had been building for a long time.

Evan was born June 8, 1878, the ninth child of strongly Calvinist parents devoted to the Lord, whose house was ruled by the Bible and prayer.[10] That home was near Loughor, in southeast Wales. In 2014, Loughor was listed among Wales's most desired residential communities, but in 1878 it was a country village, not sophisticated even by the standards of that time and probably not known much beyond.

The river Loughor wound its way through the region. When heavy rains pelted the area, the river would rise and flood what locals called "the island." In fact, Evan's boyhood home was nearby and was called the Island House. Normally the ground closer to the river's east bank was above water, but unusually high tides as well as floodwaters would douse a nearby meadow where Evan and his siblings played during dry spells.

Evan's interests were wide-ranging. He loved to contemplate the sky and the universe beyond it. Geology fascinated him. He enjoyed writing poems and music, learned shorthand, and even showed interest in the "occult sciences."[11] But as H. Elvet Lewis wrote, Evan was characterized by a "quiet strength" that compelled people around him not to curse or speak in a vulgar way.

Evan was nurtured in the faith, and that faith grew as his lanky body also developed. Each Sunday the family walked the two-mile roundtrip to their church several times. Once a friend talked to Evan about how financial challenges kept some people from going forward in Christian ministry. "God will raise great instruments for it from the mines and fields," Evan replied. He expressed hope that God would raise up a great reformer in Loughor, a person like Paul, "to set the place on fire."[12]

REMEMBER THOMAS

In 1891, at age thirteen, Evan joined the Moriah Calvinistic Methodist Church.[13] A deacon challenged him immediately about the importance of maintaining strong faith. "What if the Spirit were to come down and you were absent?" he asked. "Remember Thomas, what a loss he suffered." Evan looked at the man and perhaps did not know how to answer; however, inside, he was thinking, *I will have the Spirit.*

The little church, like Loughor, seemed insignificant, yet it would become crucial in calling down the revival lightning. The importance of Moriah Chapel and Loughor is reflected in an observation by David Matthews:

When the revival burst forth in all its glory within the walls of Moriah Calvinistic Chapel, the unsophisticated inhabitants of the smug hamlet were like them that dreamed—they seemed to have been aroused out of the sleep of ages. Staggered by the strange, unheard-of sights, they wondered what was happening. Before they had completely recovered from surprise, the name of the village, Loughor, had become famous overnight.[14]

Organized in 1739, the small Moriah congregation met initially in a farmhouse kitchen. Not long after Rev. Hopkin Bevan became its pastor, the church began to grow and needed a larger building, but the people did not have the money. Elizabeth Morgan, however, left funds in her will for the renovation of a thatched barn for the church. Thus in 1827 or 1828 the people met in what would be called the "thatched roof chapel."

In the latter half of the nineteenth century the church began to grow again. In 1898 a larger building was erected. Pastor Daniel Jones preached the dedicatory sermon on a July Sunday in 1899, centering on a single verse: "The LORD our God be with us, as he was with our fathers: let him not leave us, nor forsake us" (1 Kings 8:57 KJV). Perhaps Evan heard that sermon. Neither he nor Pastor Daniel Jones could possibly imagine that Moriah would be the home church of the man who would be viewed as the human leader of the Welsh Revival of 1904.

Before that special season of Evan's life, there would be intense preparation through experiences that seemed to have little or nothing to do with the work God would use him to accomplish.

ZONE OF EXCELLENCE

Evan Roberts, like all of us, had what I call a "zone of excellence." Imagine an area marked off within a large pasture, and a farmer plants special fruit-bearing crops inside that area. The best fertilizers nurture the ground there. The soil is richer than any other field on the farmer's land. Water is abundant. The farmer knows that anything planted inside that zone will flourish and the fruit harvested from that area will always be excellent.

The zone of excellence is a region of our lives and work where whatever we do succeeds excellently and failure appears impossible. There are four specific boundaries that define the zone: our identity in Christ, our spiritual gifts, our talents and skills, and the suffering that hones and matures us in faith and ministry.

Some see suffering as mere fate, with no outcomes other than misery. This is not the way that Jesus or those in Christ see their pain. Instead, there is purpose in suffering. It is a means of shaping their souls, linking their identities in Christ, their spiritual gifts, their talents and skills in service to others that points people to God, just as the Lord did during His incarnation in the material world.

And so it was that Evan Roberts passed through many seasons of suffering.

It began early in his life. Henry Roberts, Evan's father, was a coal miner. In 1889, Henry broke his leg in a mining accident. He could not afford to miss work, so he struggled on, limping every step. Henry finally knew he needed help to perform his tasks as a pump man, so he took eleven-year-old Evan out of school, and the boy became his father's assistant.

"Evan's brief morning of childhood was over as he put on the tough clothing of a collier, collected his personal lamp at the pithead and went down into the depths," wrote Brynmor Pierce Jones.[15] By the time Evan was twelve, his father had fully recovered. Evan now took his own job in the mine: doorboy. He sat in the dark tunnels and opened and closed the ventilation chambers and gates as the hefty coal carts made their journey down the pits. The darkness was punctuated only by the miners' lamps. Evan spent his days looking at those little points of light and listening for the clatter of drams. Otherwise his underground workstation was dark and silent.

A caravan of heavy-laden coal cars once broke loose. They plunged down an incline toward Evan. He managed to jam himself into a small space between the pit wall and the tracks on which the cars moved toward the bottom of the pit. They whooshed by Evan, barely leaving him unscathed, though just a small gap kept him from being crushed by the drams. Evan faced much danger in the mines, but he seemed to have protection through it all. Some of the miners began to think there must be a special hand guarding Evan.

Evan's protection was demonstrated again in January 1897. An explosion at the Broadoak colliery killed five miners and set off a fire in the pit. But Evan was not there because the event did not happen on his shift. When Evan heard about the accident, he thought about his Bible. He had found a slight crevice in the rock wall where he could store his Bible while he worked. As soon as he could, Evan searched for the Bible. He found it tinged with scorch marks but still readable. A century after the experience, the displayed Bible still bears the scars from the fire.

God also was working in the boy's heart, and it was in the midst of all this that Evan decided to join Moriah Chapel. He soon became intensely involved, constantly attending prayer meetings and Bible studies. One of the growing themes of his intercessions was for revival. "For ten or eleven years I had prayed for revival," he wrote years later. "I could stay down all night reading or speaking about revivals. It was the Spirit who was at that time moving me to speak of revival."[16]

In 1895, Moriah opened a school at Pisgah. The church members were expected to help, and seventeen-year-old Evan stepped forward. He launched a Bible class and prayer meeting. People assumed Evan would become a minister, but he felt unqualified. "It was noticed by some of his friends that the refusal, to some degree, changed his character. . . . But the fire was burning inwardly in secret."[17]

Blacksmith's Apprentice

Evan could not see the future, thus he began to focus on a career that would free him from a life in the mines. His maternal grandfather had been a blacksmith, and it occurred to Evan this would provide the career upon which he could settle his life. He decided to learn the trade, go to the United States, set up a blacksmith shop, save his money, and return home to Wales for a quiet retirement or fund his own ministry as a traveling revivalist.

On September 18, 1902, he launched forward as an apprentice in his Uncle Evan Edwards's shop, four miles from his home. Evan entered an agreement with his uncle that the apprenticeship was for three years. He continued to ache for the coming of revival and attend prayer meetings and spend much time in intercession for revival. But the great desire for revival burning in his heart "was too strong to be suppressed by any circumstances," wrote Daniel M. Phillips in his biography of Evan Roberts.[18] Phillips knew Evan well after traveling extensively with Evan during his ministry.

Though Evan tried to learn to be a smithy, there might have been times when he looked at the vise at the shop's worktable and felt *he* was the object that was being squeezed. He could see his Bible nearby, just as it had been in the mines, yet there was little time to study. Despite his lack of training, he had begun to sense God's calling to be a minister. But the call was intensifying and some tension with it. Finally, after fifteen months, Evan could hold out no longer, yielded to God's call, and left the apprenticeship to pursue God's vocational call. His mother realized that the family owed her brother for the full three-year period to which all parties had agreed. It is a tribute to her integrity that she took funds from the family savings to pay the entire sum that had been agreed upon, though Evan was far short of the three years.

One spring night after he had made his decision to leave his uncle's blacksmith shop and commit to full-time ministry, Evan was praying at his bedside. Something happened. He described it like this:

> While on my knees I was caught up into space, without time or place—communing with God. Before then I had only a God at a distance. I was frightened that night, never afterwards. I trembled so that the bed shook. . . . After that experience I used to be awakened every night a little after one. . . . I would spend about four hours, without a break, in divine communion. . . . Then about five I would be allowed to sleep again until near nine, and then I would be taken up to the same divine communion, and so till twelve or one. . . . That lasted for some three months.[19]

During that period the process was underway that would lead to Evan becoming a candidate for ministry in the Calvinistic Methodist denomination. He would have to preach trial sermons at Moriah and other chapels and present the testimony of his conversion to Christ and his call to ministry before seasoned and wise church leaders.

Then there was the matter of schooling. Evan was uncomfortable with the notion of going to seminary. He believed such schools choked the fervency of many young preachers. Nevertheless, he accepted the fact that getting a more formal education was an essential segment of his route to church ministry, and he determined to go forward despite his reservations.

So, at age twenty-six, on September 13, 1904, Evan found himself entering Newcastle Grammar School. He had to complete his education there before he could move on to seminary.

As Evan took up residence in Newcastle, he was still concerned that adjusting to the new lifestyle and the demands of his academic work would rob him of the powerful communion with the Lord he had come to anticipate so much. So he committed a half hour each day to "this practice of the presence of the Lord," while simultaneously pursuing his school studies.[20]

Then Evan came down with a cold and was bedridden for four days. "The last night of the four the perspiration streamed down, the result of the cold and of my communion with God," he recalled.[21]

Finally, on Sunday, Evan was able to get up. He discovered that Seth Joshua was there, along with Sydney Evans and a few others from New Quay. Joshua was actually headed to Cardiganshire to conduct a mission, but there had been a change in plans, and God had sovereignly rerouted him to Newcastle. "That moment I felt the Spirit descending upon me," Evan said.[22]

On Tuesday, Evan wanted to get to the chapel for a prayer meeting. He rushed out so quickly he forgot his heavy coat. Evan thought of the young women from New Quay who were in Joshua's group and who had been touched by God's power. Evan was moved to pray for them. Yet throughout that day he also felt a hardness of heart, making prayer difficult and then impossible. The turbulence in his soul intensified. There was conflict: "I loved the Father and the Spirit, but did not love the Son," he wrote.[23]

That Wednesday, despite his personal upheaval, Evan went with the group to a third prayer meeting at Blaenannerch. They traveled some eight miles and arrived at the home of Rev. Evan Phillips, who had been among the evangelists of the 1859 revival. A prayer meeting was underway at the house, but Evan held back. He felt "as hard as flint, as if someone had swept every feeling out of him." He shared this with Magdalen Phillips, who agreed to pray for him.

Later that Wednesday evening, the New Quay women prayed and counseled with him, but the hardness persisted. Finally, Evan told them: "There is nothing for me to do but to wait for the fire to descend. The altar is ready, the wood upon it, and the sacrifice ready, only waiting for the fire to descend."[24]

And descend it did, for this was the September 29, 1904, Blaenannerch prayer meeting described at the beginning of chapter 1 where Evan Roberts was struck by the revival lightning!

FROM THE MINE OR THE PLOUGH

What happened to Evan Roberts was God's direct answer to a prayer Seth Joshua had been sending heavenward repeatedly. He asked the Lord to "raise up someone from among the people—from the mine or from the plough—not from the Colleges, lest that might seem to crown earthly pride."

From the moment the bolt of personal revival hit him, Evan knew that he must go as a revivalist. "Ever after that hour," he said later, "I was on fire to be allowed to go through the whole of Wales, and if it were possible, I was willing to pay God for the permission to go." Thus a plan was developed for a team of eight to travel through Wales to advance revival. Evan would pay all expenses—two hundred pounds if need be.

Evan had several visions that seemed to confirm his calling and anointing. On October 6, 1904, he and a few others were with revivalist Joseph Jenkins, who was leading a meeting at Twrgwyn, five miles from Newcastle. As they traveled back to Newcastle after the service, Evan told Sydney Evans of his vision that one hundred thousand people in Wales would turn to Christ.

"Do you think that it is too much to ask God to save one hundred thousand in Wales?" Evan asked.

"No," replied Sydney Evans. "It would not be too much to ask Him to save Wales and the world."

"Well, we must go after it earnestly," Evan said.

They arrived at Twy Llwyd, Evan's home in Newcastle, at 1:00 a.m. Rather than going to bed, Evan lingered in the garden, his spirit and soul churning. Then there was a burst of inner light, and he hurried to the bedroom where Evans was already sleeping. Evans woke up and stared into Evan's face, which was aglow.

"Sid, I have got wonderful news for you!" Evan said. "I had a vision of all Wales lifted up to heaven. We are going to see the mightiest revival that Wales has ever known—and the Holy Spirit is coming just now. We must be ready. We must have a little band and go over all the country preaching. Do you believe that God can give us one hundred thousand souls now?"

At one point, perhaps looking out the bedroom window or strolling in the garden, they were aware of the intense brightness of the moon in those wee hours of the morning. Both men suddenly saw a vision. An arm stretched from the moon to earth. To Evan's and Sydney's hearts this was confirmation that God would indeed give them one hundred thousand converts—which was exactly what happened over the next six months.

Years later, on the golden jubilee of the revival, Sydney Evans described the experience. The place and the moment seemed surreal, strange. He remembered asking Evan what he was seeing. The answer came at the moment Sydney asked: he saw the arm reaching from the moon just as Evan was seeing it.

On October 28, 1904, Evan would have another encounter with the Holy Spirit, one that would be definitive and transformational. Joseph Jenkins, another great revival preacher, was leading a meeting at Capel y Drindod. Evan was present and roiling inside because the people seemed to be caught up in themselves and not focusing on or glorifying Jesus. When the service was over, he and Sydney walked back to Newcastle. They were heavy with the burden for men and women to know God, and they prayed through the night for the salvation of people everywhere.

Suddenly there was a breakthrough of the Holy Spirit. "At last the promised infilling of the Spirit," Evan recalled. "The divine outpouring was so heavy that I had to shout out and ask God to withhold His hand."[25]

Evan was excited as Sunday, October 30, 1904, dawned. He went to Bethel Chapel, Newcastle. The preacher's text that morning was "Father, glorify Thy Son." Evan took in the words, which were a balm to him. He softly said to himself: "This place is full of the Holy Spirit . . . I can feel Him blowing." Rachel Phillips was in a nearby pew and said, "It was a Sunday to be remembered." She could not hold back the tears throughout the service, which was characterized by a "silent influence . . . touching the strings of the heart." She couldn't see Evan's face directly, but others said it was glowing. Rachel, however, could see that Evan's "countenance was changing" and looked like he was "under a wonderful influence."[26]

The focus of the afternoon prayer meeting was the theme set during the morning service: "Father, glorify Thy Son."

There was a crescendo throughout that Sunday, building toward some special moment.

The evening service had a new theme: "Father, the hour has come." Rachel Phillips noted that Evan seemed to lose awareness of everything around him. He "was absorbed into communion with

God," she wrote. In that communion, Evan suddenly knew he must leave Newcastle and the grammar school and return to Loughor. He saw in his spirit the Sunday school room in Loughor. And a voice whispered in his ear, "Go to these people."

Kronos and Kairos

The entire experience through which Evan Roberts passed that Sunday and the previous months shows how *kronos* and *kairos* work in God's sovereign plan in the lives of His servants. We discussed the nature of time according to the biblical view in a previous chapter, and now we observe it in Evan Roberts's experience. He had been moving in sometimes frustrating, slow, seemingly meaningless *kronos* time. Now, however, it is apparent he had been on the track all along that would take him into the *kairos*, the special season for which God had predestined Evan.

In the wake of this calling to go home to Loughor and to launch out from there, Evan's focus on his schoolwork became impossible. He prayed and wept all day and into the night, crying out for a movement of the Spirit upon Wales. He was in a state of soul travail, and those who watched often could not understand what they were seeing. Some thought he was losing his mind. The pull of unconditional and total surrender to the revival call was intense within Evan, and he earnestly wanted to yield. He knew he had to follow the road back to Loughor, and that meant withdrawing from school.

In the intuitions of the Spirit, Evan knew the way a person left one place to go to another was important. He recognized he could not just disappear from Newcastle and the school as if he had vanished in the night. How could he handle this leaving?

Evan was blessed by the fact that John Phillips, the principal, was a man who walked in and by the Spirit of God. He had encouraged the students to attend the revival services, even if it meant missing their studies. In a letter to Florrie Evans, who had experienced the revival lightning even before Evan Roberts, Evan told of his encounter with the principal:

> I told Mr. Phillips that I failed to have quietness in Chapel, and I asked whether it was the Spirit or the devil that was working. Mr. Phillips said unhesitatingly—"O, the Holy Spirit was working, and it will be beneficial for you and them [the young people at Loughor] to be together for a week.[27]

Evan knew that missing a week from his preparatory studies would end his student career, including the possibility of going to college or seminary. But he also knew that he had to go back to Loughor. Even his principal had borne witness to that.

The next morning, October 31, 1904, Evan was on the platform at the Newcastle station, awaiting the 10:45 a.m. train to Loughor to organize the young people at Moriah to pray for and proclaim revival throughout the region and ultimately all of Wales.

Evan Roberts was a man who had experienced the living energy and radiated it across the land. But even before the bolts struck him, there were others who were already being energized by the power of God. They were the lesser lightning rods that drew revival to Wales in 1904.

CHAPTER 9

Many Rods

*The dynamic of revival lies in these
small clusters of earnest souls.*
—ROBERT COLEMAN[1]

Evan Roberts himself acknowledged he was not the only person to call down revival lightning. Sydney, Australia's *Smith's Weekly* newspaper quoted Evan: "I am not the source of this revival. I am only one agent in what is going to be a multitude. . . . I am not the one who is moving men's hearts and changing men's lives. Not I, but God working in me."[2]

People in the twenty-first century can learn much from the revival that fell upon Wales at the beginning of the twentieth century. One of the vital lessons is that the move of God in Wales in 1904–1905 was not a series of celebrity events. Evan Roberts would become famous, and people would say, "There he is!" as he entered churches, but that cloak of fame did not fit him, and he constantly tried to shake it off.

In today's celebrity culture there is the tendency to try to put it on. The fame frenzy stoked by the Internet and selfie culture is driven more by narcissism than the Holy Spirit. The quest for celebrity status—intended or subconscious—in the religious world may be actually quenching revival in our times.

Emily Esfahani Smith captured the contemporary *zeitgeist* when she wrote that many people today "think that living a meaningful life requires doing something extraordinary and attention-grabbing like becoming an Instagram celebrity, starting a wildly successful company or ending a humanitarian crisis."

However, Smith said she's learned that "the most meaningful lives . . . are not the extraordinary ones. They're the ordinary ones lived with dignity."[3]

Unvisited Tombs

Emily Esfahani Smith sees an example in Dorothea Brooke, the heroine in George Eliot's novel *Middlemarch*. Dorothea's life begins in wealth, and she wants to be a philanthropist. Instead, her life's journey takes her into what seems to be the unexceptional and humdrum, and her youthful dreams of being a notable person are shattered. She is a "foundress of nothing."

Yet rather than becoming a pack rat of bitterness and memories of regret, Dorothea determines to make a contribution with what she is and what she has at that moment:

Her full nature, like that river of which Cyrus broke the strength, spent itself in channels which had no great name on the earth. But the effect of her being on those around her was incalculably diffusive: for the growing good of the world is partly dependent on unhistoric acts; and that things are not so ill with you and me as they might have been, is half owing to the number who lived faithfully a hidden life, and rest in unvisited tombs.

So there were many lightning rods in Wales prior to the emergence of Evan Roberts who passionately sought God to send down the lightning. Many of them are those who did indeed live "faithfully a hidden life" and whose remains "rest in unvisited tombs."

There were small and obscure churches and towns that were already thriving with the revival before Evan Roberts's arrival—like Treharris, where nine hundred people made decisions for Christ two weeks before Evan visited, and Tylorstown, where revival happened a month before Evan's coming. Other places like Morriston, Glamorgan, and Monmouthshire were also experiencing the lightning before Evan's visitation.[4]

"Already the meetings were being carried on by the people themselves, sometimes with pastors present, and sometimes without them," noted Keith Malcomson as he surveyed the history of the Welsh Revival. By the time the revival movement emerged, "There were approximately 40,000 believers who had become utterly desperate for God to pour out His Spirit in Wales." The Holy Spirit "was beginning to link them together in order to release one of the great demonstrations of the mighty power of God in answer to their prayers."[5]

There should be no disparagement of Evan's role, for through him and the move of God at Moriah Chapel the outbreaks of revival here and there coalesced into a movement. Yet it is important to reflect upon a few of the other people also used of God to call down the lightning.

W. S. Jones

"Remarkably, the first known spark of the work of God that became the Welsh Revival took place in Scranton, Pennsylvania," wrote Rick Joyner.[6]

W. S. Jones was a Welsh pastor who played a major role in the linking of individuals and groups in Wales interceding for revival. He had been called in the closing years of the nineteenth century from his native land to America to become pastor of a Welsh Baptist church in Scranton. Jones seemed to be a master of the *hwyl*, that style of Welsh oratory that dazzled congregations with its intellect and polished oratory. But in 1898, despite larger crowds filling the pews in his church, the Holy Spirit led Jones into a season of spiritual crisis. Joyner said that "suddenly he became broken before God and he saw that he was not a true prophet of the New Testament type." Jones awoke to the stark reality that he had been preaching to impress people rather than to bring forth the fruit of the kingdom in their lives individually and as congregations.

This awareness shattered the pastor. He sought the Lord with intensity, and the Holy Spirit responded by striking Jones with the lightning of personal revival during a meeting led by followers of the American evangelist Dwight L. Moody.

In Joyner's words, Jones's "eloquence had been replaced by passion."

But with the bolt of revival lightning came a shift of focus and a new call. Jones's eyes were turned back to Wales and the needs of his native land for a great move of God. He resigned the thriving Scranton congregation and crossed the Atlantic to take up his mission to help bring revival to his home country.

At the opening of the twentieth century Jones was at Carmarthen in Wales. The Holy Spirit continued to keep the revival fire burning in his heart and even manifested divine healing in his body for a chronic condition. There was already a spiritual stirring in the principality through people like Joseph Jenkins. Jones was used of God to impact a region south of Tonypandy, at Clydach Vale. Meanwhile, revival fires blazed then smoldered then flared in other parts of Wales.

At Penuel Chapel in 1900, in Evan Roberts's hometown of Loughor, Jones experienced another infilling of the Holy Spirit. Here he received the physical healing referred to above and a new focus in preaching: holiness brought by surrendering to Jesus Christ. A new passion surged in Jones's spirit and soul to spark intercession for revival among other pastors. In 1903–1904, Jones organized prayer gatherings with ministers, aimed specifically at asking God for revival in Wales. They saw God's answers to those prayers among the young people in Penydarran and Pencoed. The youth meetings swelled, and many joined them in seeking God for revival.

The fire spread throughout the Rhondda Valley, creating "the tinder-dry, combustible atmosphere which so readily burst into flame in November 1904, causing many in the mining communities there to be born again and added to the chapels."[7]

W. S. Jones was an important rod calling down early strikes that would lead to the major bolt in late 1904.

FLORRIE EVANS

No doubt W. S. Jones was a key person in the period leading up to the revival of 1904–1905, but Florrie Evans, according to David Edward Pike, a historian of the revival, "is generally regarded as having sparked off the Revival in a Calvinistic Chapel in a small seaside community in West Wales."[8]

Though only a teenager at the time, Florrie Evans, said Pike, is "arguably" one of the "highly significant figures" in the revival. Florrie ultimately became part of the initial group Evan Roberts assembled after he left school at Newcastle Emlyn and returned to Loughor to get ready to spread revival fire throughout Wales.

She had been brought up in New Quay, whose proximity to the sea meant that its harbor was full of fishing boats. The village in the years of her childhood was dotted with fishermen's thatched houses. Here and there sea captains' "imposing terraced houses" rose elegantly over the port.[9] The little place bustled with shipbuilding and its attendant industries, blacksmith shops, and fishing.

Churches were scattered through the town. Pike wrote:

> In this little place . . . one of the most momentous moves of the Holy Spirit began that has ever hit Wales, spreading eventually not only across the entire county of what was then Cardiganshire, but right across Wales, and beyond to some other parts of the United Kingdom and even to some of the furthest reaches of the entire globe.[10]

Florrie Evans seems to have been the rod that called down that lightning in early 1904, months before many in Wales would awaken to the fact that 1904 would be one of the most important years in their country's history. Rev. Joseph Jenkins was pastor of New Quay's Tabernacle Calvinistic Methodist Chapel, Florrie Evans's home church. At the beginning of 1904, Jenkins was passing through a spiritual crisis. He sought God intensely in prayer, and suddenly one night he was struck by the power of the Holy Spirit and his entire ministry changed.

Young people in the church were among the first to be affected by this bolt of revival. Nineteen-year-old Florrie had not professed

Christ publicly, but with her family, she had gone to Tabernacle Chapel through the years. On February 14, 1904, Jenkins preached from 1 John 5:4: "For whatsoever is born of God overcometh the world: and this is the victory that overcometh the world, even our faith" (KJV). Florrie was pierced with the truth, ministered through the fresh anointing that had come upon Pastor Jenkins. She stayed behind and sought counsel from the pastor and later talked more with him at his home.

Jenkins urged Florrie to give her life to Christ as Savior and Lord. He advised her to return to her room at home and remain there. After the brief walk to her house, Florrie followed Jenkins's guidance. She yielded her life to Christ and "determined from that point on to obey as far as she could any promptings she received from the Holy Spirit."[11]

The next Sunday, Florrie remained at the church after the evening service with about sixty—mostly young—people to receive special catechetical instruction from Jenkins. "What does the Lord Jesus Christ mean to you?" he asked them.

"He is the Savior of the world!" a young man replied.

Jenkins, wanting to probe the heart and not just the head, asked the question again. This time he emphasized what Christ means to *you*.

There was silence as the people pondered the question.

There was a buildup in Florrie's mind and heart. She focused on capturing and communicating the words that would describe the indescribable—the experience she had had the previous Sunday in her room.

Finally, she stood and said, "I love the Lord Jesus with all my heart!"

"With that the floodgates opened."[12] The room was quiet, heavy with the sincerity and simplicity and profundity of the confession.

Sobbing was heard as others received in their hearts the penetrating declaration from Florrie's heart.

Conviction spread audibly and tangibly in the form of more weeping and confession. The Spirit-given sense of God's love through Jesus Christ changed the very atmosphere of the place.

In the days ahead, Tabernacle Chapel underwent a transformation. The youths constituted the core of the new flame of passion for Christ there. Jenkins was a visionary pastor and saw more in what was happening in his church than just the local. He organized the young people to go to other congregations and call down the lightning. Across the county, spiritual renewal began to pulsate in the churches as young people testified and sang and Jenkins preached under the renewed power he had experienced earlier.

"Effectively that was the start of what came later to be known as the Welsh Revival," Pike concluded.[13]

Joseph Jenkins

Joseph Jenkins, Florrie Evans's pastor at New Quay, was a Cardinganshire native who was "born in the heat of the 1859 revival," wrote Eifion Evans.[14] His whole upbringing was immersed in the ethos of that age.

Lamentations 3:27 particularly moved him. Its admonition seemed to speak directly to him:

> It is good for a man that he should bear
> The yoke in his youth.

At the time, the Salvation Army was very active in the Rhondda Valley where Jenkins, as a teenager, was apprenticed to a tailor who shared a deep faith in the Lord. The focus of the preaching of the Salvation Army teams was the spiritual and moral decadence of the age. The memory of these faithful and courageous people was seared into young Jenkins's soul, and he felt God's call on his own life.

After his ordination, Jenkins served a congregation at Caerphilly and then Liverpool. After three years at Liverpool, he became pastor of the church in New Quay, where Florrie Evans attended. Jenkins's nephew, John Thickens, was the minister of Tabernacle Chapel, Aberaeron. The two men spent much time together, discussing their mutual concern for the deteriorating spiritual situation in the regions where they worked. They were no doubt picking up on the concerns that prompted David Howell to write his letter of urgent concern at the close of 1903. In addition to his concerns about the theological drift into liberalism, Howell, a widely respected senior churchman, declared that revival was the only hope for the society: "Spiritual revitalization! . . . Not a local disturbance . . . but a kind of spiritual saturation, that overflows into the country as a whole, that would immerse all classes with the Baptism of the Holy Spirit . . . the only source of spiritual life." Howell concluded, "It is not possible to produce or revive religious life by any means apart from the instrumentality of the Spirit." He quoted Zechariah 4:6: "'Not by might, nor by power, but by my Spirit,' saith the LORD of hosts."[15]

Jenkins and Thickens shared Howell's passion. Interactions with men and women who had been affected by the Keswick movement (also known as the Higher Life movement, which pursued Christian holiness in England) both encouraged them and stirred an even greater desire for the kind of revival Jenkins remembered from 1859.

To their minds, there seemed to be a "veneer of formality that was stifling church meetings," wrote historian R. Tudur Jones.[16]

Jenkins and Thickens yearned to see services characterized by spontaneous singing, testifying, and praying. In October 1903, Jenkins tried such an approach and felt the "first signs of sunrise from on high were seen."[17] Among other things, an elder came forward, deeply moved after hearing a young person pray. As he wept, the man said: "It is all right. I know him. He is the Holy Spirit."

There was also much stirring in Jenkins's spirit and soul. In 1903, he had moved from a mere religious commitment to God's assurance of his personal salvation. On one occasion as Jenkins and a close associate, Ceredig Evans, wept and prayed together, Jenkins heard the voice of the Spirit telling him to "fulfil his ministry." On another evening, alone in his study, Jenkins experienced a vision of the cross that saturated him with joy and peace.[18]

This was the situation into which Florrie Evans stepped when she made her confession of love for Christ at the youth meeting at Tabernacle Chapel where Jenkins was pastor.

JOHN PUGH

Florrie Evans, perhaps from the perspective of her childhood in the late nineteenth century, might have concluded that quiet and quaint New Quay was the picture of all Wales. But there were things stirring in urban areas that also were changing the face of her country.

John Pugh understood the transformations, saw their promise and also the large-scale problems arising from them, and he dedicated himself to doing something about it. This Calvinist Methodist minister was already hard at work, not knowing that in 1904 he would be used of God to crucially influence the shape of the revival.

In the last decade of the nineteenth century a whole new sector of Welsh society was developing. Bucolic farms were shrinking and even disappearing, along with small shops and home-based enterprises. Steelworks, docks, and railroads were being built and expanded. New mines and quarries were being carved out of the rock face and into the depths of the land. Urbanization was underway, with cramped housing, inner-city misery, crime, drunkenness, and prostitution all in the midst of the wealth to be gleaned from the bustling industries.

A new demographic category was emerging. The Welsh language was the *patois* of rural Wales, but English increasingly was the *lingua franca* of the urban centers. The Calvinistic Methodists who would be at the center of the revival lightning were based primarily in the countryside, with little interaction and understanding of the needs of the English-speaking cities.

That is, except for John Pugh, a Calvinistic Methodist leader.

Pugh could relate to the scrappy urban lifestyle and the ruffians who pursued it. He had been rebellious in his youth, but when he was converted to Christ while he was still in his teens, he came into the kingdom earnestly and abandoned defiant, unruly behaviors. Pugh joined the Calvinistic Methodist denomination in which his parents had raised him. Eventually he became a successful church planter as leader of what became known as the Forward movement. But that was years into his future.

Now, as he grew physically, a passion for reaching the unsaved grew as well. Soon he was organizing teams to conduct outdoor evangelistic rallies. Pugh entered Trevecca College at the age of twenty-three. He took up his first pastorate at Tredegar, a town humming with industrial fervor as a new mining center.

Always edgy, Pugh decided to take his church outside and began holding services in front of the town hall. Opposition developed quickly from people within his church who felt he was marring the church's dignity. But Pugh pressed on. Within nine years the Tredegar congregation swelled from sixteen to four hundred.

He then went on to Pontypridd, where he planted a new church in a rented room inside the town school. But once again he felt the pull to reach the hard to reach. Pugh began holding services in the town square, which was surrounded by seventeen pubs. Many were converted, pub profits plummeted, and some of the bar owners paid hooligans to harass him and a brass band to drown out his preaching. Pugh held out, knowing the horn blowers would run out of air and pause every now and then for a breath of air. He said, "When they puffed, I preached."[19]

The most important work Pugh did in Pontypridd would impact Wales and the world beyond. It was he who organized a service that would be used of God to change the life of a man whose temperament was very much like that of Pugh before he met Christ.

The man was Seth Joshua.

SETH JOSHUA

Seth Joshua would be a key person for Evan Roberts. It was Seth who had prayed the "Bend me!" prayer in Blaenannerch on September 29, 1904, that God used to ignite Evan.

Seth had good reason to pray that prayer. He himself had been bent and "saved from a life of profligacy," according to David Matthews.

Seth was born in Pontypool in 1858 and worked there as a cleaner in the sheds of the Great Western Railway. His assertive personality and athletic abilities drew other young men to him, and Seth drank and gambled with his friends. He was noted as a tough fighter and won most of the races in which he vied. He abstained from alcohol when racing. Seth also became a hard-to-beat boxer with a reputation for resilience.

Later in life Seth said, "When I look back upon it, I think of the grace that stooped so low to pick me up. . . . Do not ask me whether I ever saw a tear in mother's eye. I saw hundreds. I was going headlong over mother's tears and the billow of father's prayers. How glad I am that mam and dad lived long enough to see my return home."[20]

That return home came one day as he passed an old building where his brother Frank—already a preacher—was conducting a service in concert with John Pugh. A friend, Dai Caravan, saw Seth and dashed out to him.

"There's a revival meeting here, Seth," said Dai. "Your brother Frank was praying for you just now."

Seth was shocked and embarrassed. "Praying for me in public?" he asked. "Let him pray for himself in public, not me!"

Seth then announced his intention to continue on to a theater.

"Perhaps you will get happy in here," replied Dai. "Come on in."

Seth relented and entered the old mansion. Inside he found the people pulsating with energetic joy. They were dancing and leaping, and some were shouting, "Thank God, I am saved!"

Seth scanned the crowed and realized he knew every person there. They were regarded by some as the scum of their community. Seth saw muscular young men who had been his opponents in pugilistic matches.

Then the voice of a small girl rose in the midst of the din. She was singing:

> I'm but a little pilgrim,
> My journey's just begun;

They say I shall meet sorrow
Before my journey's done.
The world is full of trouble,
And suffering they say,
But I will follow Jesus
All the way.

Her words were like bullets, piercing Seth. "I am going to Hell!" he shouted. He was urged to go to his knees along with others who were repenting. Seth, however, told them to get away, not to lay a hand on him. They would regret it if they did, he warned. He was raging. "The devil was having his last kicks," he later said. Finally, he walked to the front of the room and knelt by a rickety chair, his heart broken in repentance. He felt light, like a huge burden had been taken off his shoulders.

Dai Caravan could see a pool of tears where Seth had stood. Seth collapsed on his bed that night, without supper, and in the morning, he awoke to a new world. He could feel the change as he headed for work. "Birds never sang as they did that morning," wrote T. Mardy Rees, one of Seth Joshua's biographers. "The springtime of grace had entered his soul."[21]

Later that evening Seth passed a hangout where his friends loitered. "Seth, come have a drink," one called out.[22]

"Boys, I have found another well," he replied. "Come, and have a drink of it."

From that moment, Seth never looked back. "Seth Joshua was every inch a 'man of God,'" wrote Matthews. "Every heartbeat had been dedicated and concentrated to the service of the Highest."[23]

This was the man God used to lead Evan Roberts under the cloud, positioned for the lightning.

Sydney Evans

Sydney Evans was to Evan Roberts what Barnabas or Silas was to the apostle Paul—and even more. Neither of Paul's companions might be described as the apostle's best friend, but Sydney was often characterized as such in relation to Evan.

This was exceptional in light of Evan's personality and preferences. He was "a private man, keeping everyone at arm's length," wrote R. Tudur Jones, a historian of Welsh religion and culture. The only people with whom Evan had a close relationship were those in his family, the young women singers on his revival team, and Sydney Evans.

The two met at the preparatory school in Newcastle, and there Sydney played a significant role in Evan's life and work. It was Sydney who encouraged Evan to go to the 1904 meeting in which Seth Joshua uttered the "Bend me!" prayer that captured Evan's heart and led ultimately to Evan's involvement in the revival that was already underway.

On that September day Evan had been laid up with a cold, but Sydney attended the Monday meeting and excitedly reported it to Evan. The Holy Spirit was moving powerfully, and there were young women present from New Quay in Cardinganshire, where the revival lightning had struck the previous February. The glow in Sydney Evans, along with the report of the meeting, spurred Evan's desire to attend the services despite his illness.

It was not only a significant beginning for Evan but for Sydney as well.

Just how crucial Sydney was—and the degree to which Evan trusted him—was apparent in the fact that Evan would sometimes turn over leadership of the revival meetings to Sydney. During one mission, for example, Evan gave Sydney full responsibility for the meetings in Llanelly, Swansea, and Cardiff, all of which were significant locales in the revival. Llanelly was challenging, but Sydney pressed on, and then, in November 1904, he traveled to Morriston where he had a victorious campaign.

Sydney seemed to be especially anointed in leading revival services in the industrial areas. This provides an important insight into his personality. He felt comfortable going into the tough and gritty collieries, steel mills, quarries, and ports. Sydney's effectiveness in these missions was revealed in one place where members of the Union of Steel Founders, who had been impacted under Sydney's ministry, requested that alcoholic beverages be taken out of their recreation areas. An outcome of Sydney's Newport steelworks mission was the scheduling of regular breakfast-time services.

Perhaps the most important role Sydney played was as a prayer partner, and—it may not be too much to say—pastor to Evan. Sydney listened to Evan spill out the turbulence in his soul. In a later chapter we will discuss the weight of God's glory resting upon Evan, a mere mortal, and its effects. It was Sydney, Evan's friend, whose pastoral heart gave solace to Evan's weary soul when the burden of revival leadership became especially heavy.

Historian Tudur Jones said that Sydney played "a prominent part in the revival."[24] That's exactly what happened.

We have focused here on just a few of the people who were crucial in drawing the initial lightning bolts of the revival. But there are many others: nameless men and women at Treharris, in Glamorganshire, where, by January 18, 1905, nine hundred people had given their lives to Christ.[25]

We could talk about many individuals who were used of God in significant roles in the buildup and during the revival. There was D. M. Phillips, author of Evan Roberts: *The Great Welsh Revivalist and His Work*, who "wrote so much about the revival, [but] he was not tempted to draw attention to his own considerable contribution to it." In fact, the church he served as pastor in Tylorstown was experiencing revival a month before Evan's arrival there. Certainly we would need to contemplate the work of R. B. Jones, Maud Davies, Rosina Davies, and so many others.

They would be among the rods God used to call down lightning in 1904–1905. The tallest were what people deemed the lowest and least consequential in the whole society. David Matthews, who experienced the Welsh Revival, wrote:

> Insignificant occurrences are sometimes advance intimations of earth-shaking events. Sometimes we find that infinitude lies buried within the bosom of a trifle. When a "still small voice" whispered to Augustine, "Take, and read"—such a trifling occurrence—did anyone dream that the Church of God was about to be honored with one of the most brilliant preachers of all time? Did Wesley have a premonition, as he sauntered into that unadorned Moravian church in London's Aldersgate Street to hear pious Peter Bohler read Luther's commentary on Romans, that something would happen, ultimately sending a thrill of new life throughout Britain, and later, throughout the New World? Millions have since blessed God for that incident. Spurgeon found the snow so heavy upon the ground one Sunday morning that he decided to attend service in a little Methodist Church—an unorthodox thing for him to do, as he later confessed. But the unlettered local preacher had a good text that morning—"Look unto me, and be ye saved, all the ends of the earth." Whatever may be thought of the sermon, that humble unknown man was unconsciously used of God to bring into the ecclesia another Paul. Many avow that when that Spurgeon lad in his teens was brought to Christ,

the greatest preacher since apostolic days was converted. Evan Roberts crossed his Kedron to his Golgotha in a similar way.[26]

Through the "insignificant occurrences" of what popular culture deemed as insignificant men and women, God released the mighty lightning of revival upon Wales, charged with transformational dynamics.

CHAPTER 10

Dynamics of the Lightning

[Revival is] an extraordinary movement of the
Holy Spirit producing extraordinary results.
—RICHARD OWEN ROBERTS[1]

Lightning strikes the earth eight million times every day. We normally think of the bolts as destructive, but there are positive benefits as well. Lightning helps fertilize the ground by dissolving atmospheric nitrogen, which is then carried to the soil through rain. Lightning helps protect the planet as it produces ozone that provides a barrier to harmful solar rays.

Earth could not sustain life without lightning.

The spiritual lightning that will be the life energy at the heart of the great end-times revival will be the interaction between the kingdom of heaven and the domain of the created world. As life cannot exist on the planet without natural lightning, so the spiritual life of the end-times revival won't be sustained without spiritual lightning.

The incarnation of God in Jesus of Nazareth, the Christ, was the greatest incursion of heaven into the finite world, the consummate dynamic power of spiritual lightning. In many of the stories about Jesus' ministry on earth, there appears the Greek word *dunamis*, translated as "power" and from which we get *dynamite, dynamo, dynamism, dynamics,* and related words.

The great end-times revival will be the final strike of revival on earth, beginning with the great consummate strike in the coming of Jesus into the world and the continuing lightning storm through the Pentecost bolts that struck the disciples. It will be characterized by powerful spiritual dynamism and result in the transformation of individuals and societies. "These that have turned the world upside down are come hither also," shrieked the alarmed religionists at Thessalonica when the followers of Jesus came there with their power-packed message (Acts 17:6 kjv). The lightning of God's truth is upsetting, disturbing, and threatening to the perceived stability of revered institutions and the people who try to keep them standing long after their usefulness has passed.

God's Desire

One of the great desires of God's heart is that His people understand and operate in the power He imparts in the anointing of Jesus Christ made manifest through the Holy Spirit. Paul wrote, "I pray that the eyes of your heart may be enlightened, so that you will know what is the hope of His calling, what are the riches of the glory of His inheritance in the saints, and what is the surpassing greatness of His power toward us who believe" (Eph. 1:18–19).

There are actually four important Greek words encompassed here that help us understand the multifaceted nature of God's revival lightning that will be revealed again at the end of the age. As we have seen, *dunamis* refers to the capacity of power, manifested and experienced, as in a burst of dynamite or a sudden transformation. *Energeia*, from which we get *energy*, refers to the ability God places within us to work and serve and keep going in the face of weariness and trial. Among the many meanings of *ischus* are "strength for battle" as well as "strength for endurance." *Kratos* refers to "supreme might."

Evan Roberts had this fullness of God's power in mind when he wrote:

> Too weak to rise?
> Then let thy hand rest on Jehovah's arm.
> He holds creation by His mighty word.
> Too weak? Then ask,
> And take the resurrection power of Christ
> For God is able, yea, the dead to raise.
> Thou art too weak, 'tis true, but GOD!
> Is He? Nay, Nay! The Almighty One;
> The great Almighty. Yes, His power is seen
> In nature, in the heavens and all the earth.
> Glance at the stars and hear them whispering thus:
> We rest upon the power of His Word.
> Rest thou, for thou art weary and too weak.
> Rest on His Word, and let thy light go forth.[2]

The Greek words we have examined, taken as a whole, show the difference between spiritual revival and human revolutions:

- God-sent revival is transformative; human revolution is merely alterative.

+ God-sent revival is embraced; human revolution is forced.
+ God-sent revival is sustained by God's infinite transcendent authority and strength; human revolution is sustained by immanent and therefore finite human might.
+ God-sent revival lifts men and women toward God's transcendent majesty; human revolution holds people's focus on the horizontal.
+ God-sent revival is received by individuals; human revolution is coerced by those with enough muscle.
+ God-sent revival is the lightning of God's power striking in the human heart that will receive it freely and therefore works from inward to outward; human revolution is forced from outward to inward.

The powerful interactions between heaven and earth constitute the spiritual dynamics of true revival, as the Welsh experience demonstrates.

We have much to learn about the dynamos of revival as we study God's lightning that struck that land in 1904–1905. Here, then, is a sampling of the interactions between heaven and earth that brought the dynamism of revival to the little principality of Wales in the early twentieth century, which just might also be a harbinger of what we, too, will witness in the twenty-first century.

THE HOLY SPIRIT'S MANIFEST PRESENCE

Frances Schaffer wrote:

> The *central* problem of our age is not liberalism or modernism, nor the old Roman Catholicism or the new Roman Catholicism,

nor the threat of communism, nor even the threat of rationalism and the monolithic consensus which surrounds us. All these are dangerous but not the primary threat. The real problem is this: the church of the Lord Jesus Christ, individually or corporately, tending to do the Lord's work in the power of the flesh rather than of the Spirit. The central problem is always in the midst of the people of God, not in the circumstances surrounding them.[3]

Schaeffer's writings mostly focus on theology, philosophy, and culture, but he was also concerned that the church move in the manifest power of the Holy Spirit. The objectivity of the Word cannot be overshadowed by the subjective experience of its truth, but neither must the subjective be invalidated by objectivity.

Therefore, we must acknowledge the continuing objective, factual presence of the Holy Spirit and, at the same time, receive the Spirit's subjective, manifest presence. The Welsh Revival—as will the coming end-times outpouring—shows the nature of this interaction:

- The objective-factual presence is the *promise* of the presence; the subjective-manifest presence is the *presence* of the promise.
- The objective-factual presence reassures us; the subjective-manifest presence transforms us.
- The objective-factual presence is embraced by faith; the subjective-manifest presence is realized in experience.
- Faith in the objective reality of the Holy Spirit is the prerequisite for the subjective-manifest presence of the Spirit.

We must not try to force the subjective without first casting our faith utterly on the objective presence and promise of the Spirit.

This leads us to another vital spiritual dynamic seen in the Welsh Revival and what we can be assured will be forces behind the coming end-times awakening: God's sovereign will, the prayers of His people, and their relation to calling down the revival lightning.

THE INTERACTION BETWEEN GOD'S SOVEREIGNTY AND HUMAN INTERCESSION

As noted earlier, we must recognize the sovereignty of God in bringing true revival. Recall Steven Olford's observation, describing revival as "that strange and sovereign work of God in which He visits His own people, restoring, reanimating, and releasing them into the fullness of His blessing."[4]

H. Elvet Lewis experienced the Welsh Revival directly, and years later it was still on his mind. He wrote that the more the autumn of 1904 receded, "it grows more profoundly mysterious. . . . Dates, places, and persons were only outward and visible symbols of a wave-move, like a tide—nay, an overwhelming flood, that has no everyday name, no secular explanation."[5]

"We do not know how this revival originated," said Evan Roberts in one of his early meetings. In fact, he said, "We have no idea how many thousands have been praying in private for it . . . nobody knows how many."[6]

Which, then, comes first to bring revival: the intercessions of the people or the sovereign action of God?

God's sovereign will is to revive us, but He acts in the context of our free will. Therefore, God moves sovereignly on people to pray, seek His face, and repent on behalf of their land. Those people have the freedom to reject or quench the move of the Spirit to prayer, and if they do not pray, there is no lightning rod, the bolt does not come, and the cloud moves on.

Thus by the sovereign will and direction of God, the cloud comes first, and as we have seen, if there is a buildup in the ground that points where the lightning can touch—the trees, the steeples, the lightning rods, and spiritually the hearts lifted up to God that draw the spiritual bolt—then the lightning of revival will come.

So it seems that God moves His cloud sovereignly over a land and its people, because He sees the hearts there that yearn for His move upon their lives and societies. But for the bolt of reviving power to come, the people, whose hearts are stirred with the desire for His manifest presence and power, must willingly seek God.

This is the meaning and the means of calling down lightning.

Praise and Worship

The Welsh Revival also demonstrated that praise and worship are vital means of calling down lightning.

The Welsh temperament seemed attuned to music as a primary expression of praise and worship. This increased in the wake of the 1859 revival and built as the twentieth century approached. "In the second half of the nineteenth century, and with extraordinary energy, Wales turned itself into a musical nation," wrote historian R. Tudur Jones.[7]

This happened as singing festivals developed in churches—both nonconformist and conformist. Church choirs would come together at organized events on a regular basis. In addition to music, there would be a devotional focus on God's Word, along with prayer.

Church and chapel orchestras in some places were seated in front of the preaching platform, emphasizing the importance of musical praise and worship. The singing festivals were actually developing congregations in the art of raising song to the Lord, and the result was heightened praise and worship in weekly services. In fact, "the training during the singing festivals had created a musical medium suitable even for passion of a revival, as would be seen in 1904," said R. Tudur Jones.[8] The outcome was that "all this activity . . . revolutionized" congregational singing throughout the principality, he noted.[9] The Spirit-inspired expressions in Welsh Revival meetings reflected the wholeness of the adoration of the Lord, which included both *praise* and *worship.*

True praise and worship will be a vital dynamic of the end-times revival, and the Welsh Revival demonstrated it. Rev. Ilsley W. Charlton experienced the dynamics—including powerful praise and worship—of the Welsh Revival on a "cold, frosty day in a rather unattractive mining village." He was with Sydney Evans, Evan Roberts's close friend, in the small town of Ebbw Vale. Actually, Charlton had gone searching for a revival meeting and arrived at Ebbw Vale at about two that afternoon. He was going to ask someone where to go but found it unnecessary. All Charlton had to do was follow the crowds flowing in the same direction.

That tide of humanity wafted Charlton into a chapel with seating for some six hundred. Someone recognized him as a minister and ushered him to the area near the front that was reserved for church leaders. An impromptu praise and worship service started outside the chapel, and as the singing party entered, the room became packed.

Open-air praise and worship was not a contrived event. "The revival did not create the refrains that swept a vast congregation in their torrent, it found them already in the people's memory and heart—it charged them with fresh power; it sanctified them anew," wrote H. Elvet Lewis.[10]

In fact, Joseph Parry, a noted worship leader in Wales, had prophesied before his death in 1903 that the next Welsh revival—which would come just months after his passing—would be a singing revival. "I may not live to see it," he said presciently, "but some of you who are here today will see it, and you will recall my words."[11]

Charlton may not have known Parry and his prophecy, but he experienced it both inside and outside the chapel at Ebbw Vale. Once the meeting inside got underway, Charlton found:

> There was no special leader, no musical instrument, no hymn books, and no announcing of hymns. . . . Everyone was at liberty to speak, or sing, or pray if they felt led to do so—with the result that solos, choruses, hymns, prayers, praises, testimonies, of exhortations, etc., all followed one another (and sometimes went on together) without confusion of manifest disorder—perfect liberty and yet wonderful unity.[12]

The outcome in places where such a prayer and praise movement occurred in Glamorganshire as well as Tredegar was that "the whole community [became] more conscious of the divine presence and activity," with "converts . . . counted in hundreds and the favourable effects on the life of the churches . . . lasting."[13]

Arguably the single biggest change in the life of the average evangelical congregation over the past fifty years has been the sweeping movement toward a renewal in worship and the music that is played in church. Out of the choruses of the 1960s and the Jesus People movement of the 1970s came the influence of musical innovations that has continued to reverberate throughout the evangelical church ever since.

While the ensuing years saw no shortage of conflict and controversy, and the change has not come without a fight as traditionalists battle champions of the new music and worship style, there is little doubt we have entered a new era of worship that some might say has the feel of revival and is perhaps even a harbinger of the coming end-times outpouring. And like the Welsh Revival, countless multitudes worldwide have been led to Christ as a result of Holy Spirit–inspired new forms of worship and music—and they want others to know about it. This has resulted in another emphasis in contemporary worship services, namely, testimony. This was also true of the Welsh Revival.

TESTIMONY AND EXHORTATION

Testimony and exhortation are other spiritual dynamics that distinguish true revival from human-contrived religious events. They are especially powerful when linked, as they frequently were in the Welsh Revival of 1904.

To testify is to tell one's story of God's call on the individual to come out of the darkness of their lives without Christ and into His light. It reports on the activity of the Holy Spirit in transforming a child of darkness into a son or daughter of light.

Years ago I was a general assignment reporter for a large daily newspaper. This was in the era before computers and word processors, and the newsroom was a dynamic place, abuzz with the commerce of reporting the news. A police and fire department squawk box sat on the city editor's desk. Imagine that the city editor hears the dispatcher's voice reporting a great fire. The editor calls a reporter's name and tells him to cover the fire and phone in the report direct from the site.

As the reporter rushes out of the newsroom, he begins to fret about the danger of being in the middle of burning buildings. So instead of leaving the newspaper building, the reporter slips into the reference library. He pulls out an encyclopedia, writes an eloquent essay on spontaneous combustion, and plops it on the city desk. "I made deadline!" the reporter announces.

The city editor scowls as he reads the report. Then he looks at the journalist. "You are a reporter, not an essayist! I told you to go to the scene of the fire and report what you were seeing and feeling, not give me a dry paper on theory and science!"

In religious meetings there are many theological essayists. But testimony is the dynamic of revival. As a man or woman testifies he or she is *reporting* what Jesus Christ has done and is doing in their lives. They bring a story of living experience. Many Christians are reluctant to testify because they fear they will not be eloquent or theological enough.

Revival shows that God has not called us to be essayists but reporters.

Exhortation comes in many forms, for example, urging, begging, encouraging, coaching, and assuring. A major purpose of testimony should be to exhort listeners to take a new direction or make a better decision to carry out a positive and successful action and to pursue holiness and sanctification.

The power of the linkage of testimony and exhortation is that of a person sharing his or her experience with unveiled transparency and using it to encourage someone else to experience the same kind of victory, peace, and joy.

Testimony and exhortation, as we have seen, would be vital dynamics within revival services, and we are certainly witnessing a worldwide resurgence of just such spiritual phenomenon today. But they would also break out in homes, schools, athletic fields, or even workplaces. In his eyewitness account of the revival, David Matthews described how the speech and conversational topics of coal miners had changed. As they gathered at lunch breaks they would sometimes converse about revival meetings they had attended, and "the old mine would resound with their splendid voices as they testified to the goodness of the Lord."

Once a manager was making inspection rounds when he came upon miners eating from their lunch pails. He was amazed to hear these toughened men "hilariously comparing their new spiritual experiences." In fact, the change in their language and conversational topic confirmed to the manager that the miners "were speaking with 'new tongues.'"[14]

Everywhere the lightning struck, the dynamics were evident and sparked extraordinary external phenomena. Lightning can energize or it can overwhelm. Sometimes it stretched church leaders as they struggled with how to maintain order and doctrinal soundness amid the spontaneity and what on occasion felt like serendipity.

They were learning a vital principle: to benefit from the bolt of revival, church leaders must learn how to handle the lightning in a biblically sound way that does not put out the fire while making sure it doesn't burn down the house.

CHAPTER 11

Handling the Lightning

*You'll have to admit . . . that the best
place for a fire is in the fireplace, and
not out in the middle of the floor.*

—SAMUEL SHOEMAKER[1]

"God is dead" concluded Thomas Altizer, a theologian at Emory University in the late 1960s. The much-ballyhooed theory added to the tumult of that thunderous age.

Altizer's report of the death of God became sensational in the sense that a meteor flaring in the upper atmosphere is sensational for a split second before its flameout. "Is God Dead?" asked a bold red headline on the cover of *Time* magazine as Christians celebrated Christ's resurrection during Easter 1966. According to the news magazine, Altizer and a few other theologians believed "it is no longer possible to think about or believe in a transcendent God who acts in human history."[2]

I was a newspaper reporter in the 1960s, and I interviewed Altizer.

"Do you really mean that God is dead in some biological sense?" I asked.

According to Altizer (or at least my attempt at comprehending Altizer), God really did die in Christ on the cross, as the deity who transcended the material world. Through that death God became fully immanent, stripped of His supernatural status. The church, thought Altizer, keeps trying to stick God back in heaven, but that kind of being simply no longer exists, and it's impossible to breathe life back into Him.

I concluded that Altizer—and some of the other God-is-dead theologians—thought that God's death meant the deity had turned the running of the world over to humans without the consciousness of a transcendent God. For all practical purposes, God was no longer engaging with time and history and our lives within it, thus He might as well be dead.

ALIVE AND WELL

Had Thomas Altizer researched the Welsh Revival he might never have concluded that God is dead in any sense of the term. Instead, the professor would have found evidences everywhere of God's dynamic interaction with the people and institutions of Wales. Altizer would have seen that God was indeed alive and well and manifesting His presence in the British principality.

Altizer was at the flare-out of the modern age, and based on the ethos of his time, he thought people had given up on belief in the supernatural and spiritual. Ironically, he was standing at the threshold of the postmodern period, when spirituality would make a big comeback.

In 1987, two decades after Altizer and the "God is dead" move-ment, Jose Arguelles, a University of Colorado professor and art historian, declared the approach of a harmonic convergence. He had consulted ancient Mayan calendars and spoke of great beams of light from stellar sources, the unlocking of the meaning of the myth of the Mexican savior-god Quetzalcoatl, and humming and chanting by clusters of like-minded seekers around the globe in an effort to boost the vibratory rate of the planet.[3]

Arguelles also felt enlightened by the prophecies of Native American shamans and even the Bible, specifically Revelation 14:3, saying that 144,000 "enlightened teachers" should convene at centers of spiritual power around the world on August 16–17, 1987. Based on the schedule Arguelles derived from the Mayans and other ancient sources, an "oceanlike wave" would peak on those dates, bringing a "new energy and momentum" into earth in preparation for the galaxy-spanning harmonic convergence coming in 2012, as predicted by the Mayan seers. The collective chanting, visualiza-tion, and meditation by the enlightened teachers would keep the world safe in 2012, "the final stage of transformation."[4]

DISTORTION OF SPIRITUAL DYNAMICS

New Agers and spiritists of many types have latched on to and dis-torted the convergence concept, believing there are certain places on our planet where there is a harmonization of spiritual forces. The human race is full of such thought. The ancient Celts believed there were "thin places" where heaven and earth overlapped. Antiquity's Druids convened at Stonehenge—just as their modern disciples continue to do.

People across the world still bar anyone from tampering with lands and mountains and valleys that are believed to be sacred to some. Sedona, Arizona, and the surrounding landscape are sacred to many spiritists. There they find energy vortexes, healing waters, sites for building rock cairns, and labyrinths where, "as you walk you are searching within yourself for the place of Oneness where all of your answers are kept. As you walk back out you are walking your answers out into the world, creating wisdom."[5]

But as the Welsh experience shows, none of it is revival. True revival results in conviction and repentance and redemption and regeneration. Revival is not centered on making us happier with ourselves but stretched and challenged to walk in holiness and to minister more fully under the power of the Holy Spirit. Genuine revival is not a turning inward but a turning upward to God, who is "high and lifted up" and completely other.

When we talk here about spiritual dynamics and the interactions between heaven and earth in revival, we are not discussing a mere convergence of the spirits with the material world, but the visitation of the Holy Spirit, stepping into and intervening in human times, changing the lives of men and women, societies and nations, and restraining the chaos brought about by the fall.

A revival service at a small school in Wales, which Elvet Lewis attended in January 1905, shows the contrast between harmonic convergence and the actual interaction of heaven with earth in true revival. It was a sisters' meeting, with about thirty in attendance, including a few men. After prayers, there "came an indescribable moment," Lewis wrote. "There cannot be many hours in life like that hour, or part of an hour that followed. It was the spiritual world realized, actualized—to be partly lost again in the world's wintry breath, but never irrevocably lost."

Lewis hoped that "in other lands yet, in days near or far off, shall such days . . . suddenly, inexplicably, adorn some unknown year."[6]

Reversion to Paganism

Ironically, far from getting rid of the idea of the supernatural, as Friedrich Nietzsche, Altizer, and other God-is-dead proponents thought in their day, much of the planet—the West included—has reverted to the paganism that characterized the ancient world, which many believe is a sign of the end times. Sadly, this is the philosophical and metaphysical backdrop against which many now seek to understand and apply the ministry of the Holy Spirit.

Despite the bright dreams of Altizer and others for a humanity happily liberated from the deity dominating from high above, more freedom has not come. Ironically, the more irreligious and secular we have become, the more indignant and legalistic we are. Secularity, not belief in a transcendent God, is the source of the rigid political correctness of our day that is stifling free speech on university campuses, depriving bakers, wedding photographers, and others of their right to live by their beliefs and consciences. Contemporary politically correct authoritarians suffer such hubris; they believe they can redefine marriage and gender.

Under the revival, parts of Wales in 1904–1905 actually saw an easing of regulations and laws because so many people had experienced reconciliation to God the Father through Christ's regenerating dynamic and the Holy Spirit's transforming power that they no longer broke the law.

But the result of contemporary distortions of spiritual dynamics is confusion, chaos, and reactionism, even in churches. One branch of the church, fearful of emotional excesses, shuns mentioning the Holy Spirit too much, treating the third person of the Trinity almost as an intruder. Another and significant facet of the church, wanting to avoid mental and intellectual suffocation, simultaneously molds the doctrine of the Holy Spirit into postmodern spiritualism and sometimes minimizes the Father and Son with an overwrought, doctrinally unsound preoccupation with the Spirit.

THE NEED FOR BALANCE

If the church is to move forward in stabilized authority and power, she must strike a careful balance of Word and Spirit. She must anchor herself to the objectively revealed truth given in Scripture while ministering subjectively under the energy of the Holy Spirit. Without this balance, the church will either sink in a sea of dead intellectualism or perish in a wild froth of emotionalism.

Soundness of doctrine and practice is found in the balance of *orthodoxy* and *orthopraxy*. Doctrine is vital, but it must not stand alone without ministry or it becomes merely dead theology. Ministry is the goal, but if it is severed from sound doctrine, it becomes nothing more than a means of advancing personal ambition or a cover for manipulation, extending to charlatans out to enrich themselves or even pagan magic disguised as an "angel of light" (2 Cor. 11:14).

Doctrine and ministry severed from one another become ends in themselves. Ezekiel's vision of the dry bones in Ezekiel 37 shows us that there must be structure—but to what end? The point of the coming together of the bones was to provide a vehicle for the wind, the breath. Structure without content is empty and futile. The wind without structure is a ravaging cyclone destroying all in its path rather than a refreshing and energizing breeze.

The linkage of Spirit-revealed biblical doctrine and Spirit-empowered ministry is the essence of the incarnational ministry of the Lord Jesus Christ. The New Testament church, the body of Christ, thrived in that linkage and continued to impact individuals and the masses. The apostles and disciples of Jesus, in the early years of the church, seemed to live and work by a simple understanding: *if the church is the body of Christ, then the church ought to do what Jesus did in His body.*

Donald Gee noted the influence of the revival on modern pentecostalism: "Its most significant contribution was the creation of a widespread spirit of expectation: 'Faith was rising to visualize a return to apostolic Christianity in all its pristine beauty and power.'"[7] So, wrote Eifion Evans, there was an affinity between what happened in the revival generally "to the spirit of the New Testament worshipping community." Evans added:

> Here were all the ingredients: vivid experiences of the Holy Spirit's power, free and spontaneous lay participation, agonizing conviction and holy joy. In the experience of some of the converts, however, the ecstasy of the new wine was all too soon curbed by the frigidity of the old bottles.[8]

This situation caused churches struck by the revival lightning to look to the New Testament for practical guidance in handling the powerful moves of the Holy Spirit. "This reversion to New Testament order during the revival may not have been a conscious, premeditated attempt, but its affinity to early Christian practice is unmistakable," said Evans. "The absence of liturgical order or formality was based on two related ideas, the universality of spiritual gifts, and the priesthood of all believers," he wrote.[9]

THE PAGAN MIND-SET

A positive of the postmodern worldview is that it acknowledges and is open to the spiritual dimension. The negative is that the postmodern mind resists boundaries and prefers to carve out its own riverbeds, leading to destructive floods and uncontrolled excesses of belief and practice.

David F. Wells lists six characteristics of the pagan mind-set that seem to be reviving in contemporary Western culture:[10]

1. Ancient pagans believed the gods were known through nature, to the extent they were knowable at all.

2. For pagans, personal experience was the basis for understanding the spiritual.

3. According to the pagan worldview, "the supernatural realm was neither stable nor predictable," and uncertainty over the intentions of the gods led to the earthly calamity "that produced the system of appeasement represented by pagan religious rites."

4. The gods of the pagans were sexual beings, resulting in sexual overtones in the religious practices associated with them, as in "cult prostitution and an intense interest in fertility and reproduction."

5. Morality in the pagan worldview was not founded on absolutes but relative, based on the "rhythms of life" and the norms of the status quo.

6. History was without value since pagans' "lives were centered on the experience of the moment" and "experience was everything."

All this led Wells and others to conclude that the contemporary world is more like the pagan environment faced by the apostles in the first century than perhaps any period since the gospel was first preached and the church initially planted. "We today are much closer in religious temper to apostolic times than any period since the Reformation," said Wells.[11]

Many times when we hear about the signs of the end times, we talk about wars, earthquakes, famine, increased sins, and so on. We also discuss what we can do as a response to Matthew 24:14, that the gospel will be preached as a warning to all nations, which certainly gets us closer to the theme of this book—the coming move of God that will initiate a global outpouring of His Spirit and result in world-changing events. But we must also take seriously the pagan philosophies that seem to permeate every facet of society today.

The great danger is that people who are truly hungering for the Lord are vulnerable to shams and frauds. As the Judaizers Paul warned the Galatian church against or counterfeits of the work of the Spirit, like Simon the sorcerer, they seek to satisfy that hunger with warped doctrine (Acts 8:9–24). Early on, Evan Roberts was keenly aware of the need to maintain balance, and he struggled with the challenges of spiritual dynamics, knowing the careful equilibrium might be lost. But he had his critics.

FORM OR FRENZY

While Evan Roberts sought to ignore any searing criticism, he went deeper into the subjective. The issue reached a point of crisis at Cwmavon, on February 21, 1905. It happened when "Evan suddenly agonizingly declared that someone in the room was damned." At that point, people throughout the room began to pray aloud. Just as suddenly, Evan told the congregation to stop praying. There was no point in seeking the Lord for the lost person's salvation, he said, because the person was irretrievably damned.

True revival is always risky, even messy, like birth and stables. On airbrushed Christmas cards the little Lord Jesus comes from Mary's womb cleanly into a sanitized environment. Not so. The

Lord of the universe emerged from His mother amid blood and afterbirth. His birthing chamber was full of the sounds and smells of cattle and their waste. "Without oxen a stable stays clean, but you need a strong ox for a large harvest" (Prov. 14:4 NLT).

Martyn Lloyd-Jones, a careful theologian and expositor, observed:

> There are undoubtedly many problems in connection to the revival of 1904–5—certain tendencies to extreme mysticism in Mr. Evan Roberts himself, the general difference between this revival and previous revivals, and the lamentable failure of the preachers to continue preaching and teaching during the revival. . . . All revivals have produced problems—life always does—and the danger is to dismiss the entire phenomenon because of certain excesses that often accompany it.[12]

Welsh Revival meetings were anything but neat, as a gathering at Zoar Chapel in the town of Neath revealed. The building that was once Zoar Independent Chapel had been built in 1828. By 1980 it had been turned into a commercial center and in 1988 torn down. But during the fervent days of the Welsh Revival, it was one of the places Evan Roberts visited. One evening the crowd poured into the building two hours before his expected arrival. For a while the room was quiet, then an aged man began reading Scripture with such passion everyone was moved. Before he was done, others began praying. A girl's voice cried out from the balcony, begging for God's mercy. Congregational singing arose simultaneously.

Then, suddenly, someone said, "Here he comes!" Everyone turned to try to get a glimpse of Evan. He walked several steps to the pulpit, sat for a moment, face in his hands, and then he stood to speak. "The Spirit of God is not here," he said, after looking back and forth at the audience. The people were shocked. Roberts spoiled the meeting, a deacon said later, with a few others nodding in agreement.

Sometimes when things get too messy, some will try to squelch what others can see is the beginning of a move of God. Evan himself seems to have fallen into this trap. At the meeting at Zion Chapel, Cwmavon, an elderly man who was greatly respected for his character and faithfulness broke out in spontaneous prayer. After just a few words, Evan interrupted and told him to stop. "The Holy Spirit prompted the one to pray, and the same Spirit prompted others to suppress him," wrote J. Vynrwy Morgan, a critic of Evan Roberts, in a later analysis of the Welsh Revival.[13]

In this, Evan was like the Dutch boy who tried to stop a flood by putting his finger in the dike. In Evan's case it wasn't the North Sea he was trying to control but a surge of impromptu prayer he could not hold back.

David Elias, a Baptist, began to speak a prayer. Evan walked away from the pulpit and took a seat, waiting for Elias to finish. Evan sensed the congregation's "revulsion," as J. Vynrwy Morgan described it. Suddenly, Evan "fell in a heap on the floor of the pulpit, at the same time giving vent to the most doleful exclamations." The congregation seemed painfully confused.

"The flame was there, but it was extinguished," wrote Morgan.[14]

The only way to maintain a completely neat spiritual environment is to have a spiritually powerless environment. There might be strict form, but there is not likely to be the kind of revival that comes thundering in like a strong ox and results in the transformation of human beings, institutions, and societies. No doubt the dynamics of an end-times revival will be different from any previous revival, specifically as it relates to God's prophetic sovereignty. Unlike previous revivals, there will be nothing anyone can do to stop its momentum and its role in preparing the world for the return of Christ.

But in the absence of balance, there could be the frenzy of a stampede of subjectivism and emotionalism in which the oxen could impede the revival by trampling and scattering. In the midst of such an intense move of God, human leaders must maintain themselves. Mighty pressures come on the whole person—spirit, soul, and body. Exhaustion can cause a person to lose perspective and run to the extremes of either control or the lack of it. As we will see in another chapter, this imbalance was among the reasons for the Welsh Revival's fade.

ESTABLISHING EQUILIBRIUM

How can the contemporary church recapture the style and ministry of the first-century church in preparation for a great end-times awakening? Among other things, in this age of spiritual confusion and chaos, the church must not descend into chaos doctrinally or in expression. This requires delicate balances.

There are churches so mind-dependent and *objectifying* that they restrict the work of the Spirit. Martyn Lloyd-Jones noted there are those "whose whole doctrine of the Holy Spirit really leaves no room for revival."[15] There are other churches so emotion-centered and *subjectifying* that they mistake every strange phenomenon as the work of the Holy Spirit.

Closely related is the need for balance between *control* and *spontaneity*. Evan Roberts himself, especially in the latter days of the revival, seemed to want to exert control. No doubt more order was needed, but toward the end, as we will see, he became more of a controller than a leader. There are those who want to hold everything to their interpretation of Scripture while others want to move on the impulse of what they believe to be the Holy Spirit and check the Scriptures later.

Control must be replaced by strong, positive, respected leadership. Spontaneity is the subjective experience that must be limited by biblical objective boundaries. These boundaries must not themselves be subjective—that is, a matter of one's particular emotional and mental preferences—but established on the clear lines of Scripture. "Do not quench the Spirit," Paul wrote, and "do not despise prophetic utterances" (1 Thess. 5:19–20). But Paul also said that "all things must be done properly and in an orderly manner" (1 Cor. 14:40). The Greek word for "order" actually means "arrangement," "to place in one's proper order."[16] It implies thought and a degree of planning.

So, Paul said, "Pursue love, yet desire earnestly spiritual gifts, but especially that you may prophesy" (1 Cor. 14:1). He continued by providing guidelines especially for the "sign gifts" that allow for their valid expression in a nondisruptive, nonconfusing manner. Love is to guide a person's heart rather than the need to speak. At the same time it is vital that truth be uttered in the context of that love, and that truth must be given in an understandable way that does not confuse the hearers and thereby deteriorate into pandemonium.

True revival is like a beautiful orchestral performance in which there is a continual, uninterrupted flow of the core melody, with each instrumentalist free to improvise under the conductor *without playing a different song.* Thus true revival is harmony, not cacophony. The great struggle in the fallen world is between chaos and cosmos. Satan's aim in destroying anything—including revival—is to reduce it to chaos through fragmentation or to smother it in the attempt to enforce order through authoritarian suppression. Therefore the balance between form and frenzy in spiritual dynamics is crucial.

Martyn Lloyd-Jones felt that studies of the Welsh Revival—like Eifion Evans's *The Welsh Revival of 1904* for which Lloyd-Jones wrote a foreword—are important. This especially applies to periods of heightened interest in spirituality. It is important to know and recognize "the danger of passing from the spiritual to the psychological and possibly even the psychic," noted Lloyd-Jones.[17]

Establishing and maintaining healthy balance is the great challenge of spiritual dynamics. There will always be the Davids who dance so wildly before the ark that they expose their nakedness, and likewise there will always be the Michals who seek to restrain the expression (2 Sam. 6:14–16).

Working with churches across the world, whether in Europe, Asia, Africa, Latin America, or North America, I have observed the following characteristics of the kind of church that can handle the dynamics of revival and intense spiritual life in a context of biblical order.

- **Jesus-centered:** Such healthy churches understood they exist to continue the incarnational ministry of the Lord Jesus Christ. They recognize that if the church is the body of Christ, then the church ought to do what Jesus of Nazareth, the Christ, did in His body.
- **Spirit-energized:** The strong churches that can accommodate true revival realize they cannot carry out the incarnational ministry of Jesus apart from the power of the Holy Spirit any more than Jesus of Nazareth, the Christ, could during the period of His incarnation.
- **Word-anchored:** I only do what I see My Father doing, said Jesus of Nazareth, the Christ (John 5:19–23). The means by which the contemporary church can see what the Father is doing is through the Scriptures. The work of Jesus of Nazareth, the Christ, and His followers reveals the work and its nature, while the Bible as a whole shows the boundaries

that distinguish true belief and ministry as opposed to flesh-contrived ideas and actions.

+ **Kingdom-envisioned:** Churches that can handle the intensity of the revival lightning and its dynamics have a powerful vision for Christ's kingdom. They see the whole purpose of history and the church within it as the arena for the advance of the kingdom. They avoid narrow sectarianism because they see the contributions of the various parts of the body of Christ essential for the wholeness of kingdom ministry.

The revival that struck Wales in 1904–1905 stretched churches to their limits. After all, revival is the interaction between heaven and earth, the incursion of Christ's kingdom into the finite world of space, matter, and time.

CHAPTER 12

Revival and Spiritual Warfare

Behold, I have given you authority to tread on
serpents and scorpions, and over all the power
of the enemy, and nothing will injure you.

—LUKE 10:19

What might newspaper editor W. T. Stead have been thinking as he felt the *Titanic* sink beneath him on the night of
April 14, 1912? The 1958 movie *A Night to Remember* has him in
the smoking lounge, stoically facing imminent death. Or perhaps he
was clinging to a deck railing and watching the icy sea draw him in.[1]

Stead was viewed through nineteenth-century eyes as a sensa-
tionalist in journalism, what some today might call on the cutting
edge. In fact, some historians of the news business regard Stead as
a founder of investigative journalism, a style that has run the gamut
from solid, objective reporting to hysterical yellow journalism to the
fake-news classification that emerged in the twenty-first century.

On that night to remember in April 1912, perhaps Stead did a lot of remembering. As he looked down from *Titanic's* dying decks or sat grimly in the smoking room, scenes from his varied life may have played before his mind. He might have walked back through a week eight years earlier, in 1904, when he had accompanied Evan Roberts on a revival mission.

No doubt Stead's penchant for investigative journalism plus his spiritist curiosity prompted the desire to report on the revival. In addition to that, from late 1893 to early 1894 Stead had lived in Chicago. There he undertook a journalistic investigation of the seamy side of the Windy City, which was published as *If Christ Came to Chicago*.[2] In 1904, maybe he wondered what was happening when he heard Christ had come to Wales through the revival.

Stead trekked with Evan through the Rhondda Velley. He attended services there led by Evan and sipped tea with him.

In those hours in 1912 as he approached eternity, maybe Stead pulled from the sea of his own memory the conversations he had with Evan, words he scribbled in his notebook and later shared with the public. In Evan, Stead reported he had found a man who "was simple and unaffected; absolutely free from any vanity or spiritual pride."[3]

Stead had covered other revivalists and their meetings, but he had never encountered in all he knew about revival history and personal experience any "more spontaneous than this." It seemed to have "burst out here, there, everywhere, without leaders, or organization, or direction." Evan, Stead concluded, "is spoken of as the centre, . . . only because [he] happens to be one of the few conspicuous figures in a movement which he neither organized nor controls."

"The movement is not of me," Evan told Stead as they drank tea one day. "It is of God. I would not dare to try to direct it," he continued. "Obey the Spirit, that is our word in everything."

"Can you tell me how you began to take to this work?" Stead asked. Evan answered:

For a long, long time I was much troubled in my soul and my heart by thinking over the failure of Christianity. Oh! it seemed such a failure—such a failure—and I prayed and prayed, but nothing seemed to give me any relief. But one night, after I had been in great distress praying about this, I went to sleep, and at one o'clock in the morning suddenly I was waked up out of my sleep, and I found myself with unspeakable joy and awe in the very presence of the Almighty God. And for the space of four hours I was privileged to speak face to face with Him as a man speaks face to face with a friend. At five o'clock it seemed to me as if I again returned to earth.

"Were you not dreaming?" Stead asked.
"No, I was wide awake," Evan replied and then added.

And it was not only that morning, but every morning for three or four months. Always I enjoyed four hours of that wonderful communion with God. I cannot describe it. I felt it, and it seemed to change all my nature, and I saw things in a different light, and I knew that God was going to work in the land, and not this land only, but in all the world.

Evan described more about the encounter with the Lord. He spoke of his own initial concern that Satan might have been attempting to deceive him. "I went to my tutor and told him all things," Evan said, "and asked him if he believed that it was of God or of the devil. And he said the devil does not put good thoughts into the mind."

Stead concluded after his time with Evan that he "could find no trace of the devil in Wales at the present time."[4]

Whatever the case with Stead, he had landed spot-on in his observation that he had found no trace of Satan in the places he had gone with Evan. Stead, despite his own spiritual confusion, had unwittingly revealed a major component of revival, namely, its importance as a frontal assault in spiritual warfare and especially the way the spiritual dynamics of revival execute the *displacement* of the dark forces Paul referred to as the "principalities" and the "powers" (Eph. 6:12–18 KJV).

Satan and his demons seek empty places they can fill, *but so does the Holy Spirit*. Herein is the spiritual warfare of true revival. Every spiritual awakening is a lightning thrust of the filling of the Holy Spirit into places the dark spirits want as their own. Revival is a massive invasion of heaven into hell-occupied territory, a dramatic onslaught of spiritual dynamics that displaces the powers of darkness.

There may be power encounters in which exorcists go head-to-head with demons, but deliverance is sustained through displacement as the Word of God, along with praise and worship of the transcendent holy one, penetrates the demonized and pushes them back until they are crushed by the weight of God's glory.

Revival *is* spiritual warfare. The great end-times revival will be no different, but the global war will be one of greater intensity and cosmic ramifications.

REVIVAL AND DISPLACEMENT

Revival displaces the demonic and its effects because revival is the manifestation of God and His order through the power of the Holy

Spirit, bringing the ministry of the Son within the earth. God's glory, seen in true revival and expressed through intensified prayer, praise, worship, and testimony, is weightier than the kingdom of darkness.

In his vision recounted in the book of Revelation, John saw in God's right hand a sealed book. This great scroll contained the mysteries of God's work in the world. A cry went out for someone worthy to take and open the book. John wept when no one came forth "in heaven or on the earth or under the earth" (Rev. 5:3). Then one of the elders around God's throne said, "Stop weeping; behold, the Lion that is from the tribe of Judah, the Root of David, has overcome so as to open the book and its seven seals" (v. 5).

As John watched, he saw "between the throne (with the four living creatures) and the elders a Lamb standing, as if slain" (v. 6). Here is the Lord Jesus Christ, God the Son, who took the book from the right hand of God the Father. As He did, the twenty-four elders around the throne "sang a new song": "Worthy are You to take the book and to break its seals" (v. 9).

The word *worthy* used in the Greek of this passage is *axios*. The word actually refers to weight, that is, the worthy person is weighty. When God steps into a situation or place, He brings His weight to bear, displacing everything that is of less weight. Displacement is thought of frequently in relation to ships and boats afloat on water. The weight of the vessel displaces the water, a lighter substance than the wood or metal in the sailing craft, which enables floatation.

Thus, W. T. Stead was speaking more truthfully than he realized when he said that he "could find no trace of the devil in Wales at the present time."

Writing in 1957, W. E. Sangster revealed something of the displacing impact of the revival of 1904–1905 on Wales.[5] Sangster's concern in the 1950s was the deterioration in Britain at that time.

Some ask, he began, what a revival of religion might do for the country. "Nothing, it's irrelevant," some voices replied. Yet others believe revival would be "good for the masses" yet not for themselves. Thus Sangster posed the question rhetorically: "What would a Revival of Religion do for Britain?"

He answered the question by referring to the Welsh Revival of 1904.

When it first hit, "some people dismissed it all as a wave of emotional fanaticism." Ultimately, however, they changed their minds as they noted the impact of the weight of God's manifest presence in the principality.

So what would a true revival do for Britain, based on what had happened to Wales a half century earlier, along with other revivals in other times and places? What happens to any individual, group, or society impacted by true revival? Sangster described the spiritual warfare of revival's displacing influence using the following examples.[6]

1. Revival Would Pay Off Old Debts

Wherever the revival struck, "the people were paying off old and neglected and half-forgotten debts," Sangster reported. A businessman said he and his associates had scorned the news of the revival when they first heard of it. Later, though, they were of a different opinion as they noted that debts they had written off as hopeless began to be paid. "A lifting of common morality is an early and inevitable consequence of re-born religion," Sangster observed.

David Matthews wrote of his experience with the Welsh Revival. "Instances are known to me," he said, "of rent-books in arrears, and shop-books burdened with very old debts; some, indeed, had been crossed out as irredeemable by the storekeeper—completely cleared."[7]

2. Revival Would Reduce Sexual Immorality

Sangster was able to access police reports that showed 10,000 prostitutes worked in London and were visited by, on average, 250,000 men each week. "All this foul traffic is an offence to God," he wrote. "But figures and complaints will do nothing about it. A revival of religion would." The reason, he said, drawing on the evidence of revivals, is that "men and women living immorally would see that their bodies were meant to be kept in honour."

As the Welsh Revival began to spread, its displacing effects became apparent. H. Elvet Lewis noted that "somehow people who had grown gray in sin began to feel ashamed and were stricken with remorse; young people lost their taste for vacant pleasures; there were confessions, sobbings, silent tears, struggles, open victories; and the refrain grew richer as rough voices softened in singing."[8]

3. Revival Would Disinfect the Theater and the Press

Sangster said that the arts and media of his time had become so vile in some cases that one of the top reviewers, a man who did "not write from a religious angle," actually shocked performers and their audiences by walking out of a theater. He was filled with contempt "for the author's laborious filthiness of imagination." And the 1957 British newspapers "are so completely sex-sodden that they do not stop short of pornography." Revival, however, would change the landscape by leading the people "to turn from this filth in disgust, and the drama would be redeemed for its high and necessary use."

That is precisely what happened in Wales during the revival. In Aberdare, for example, "theater-going dropped markedly," reported David Matthews. "Theater-fans, scarcely ever missing a single play, found their interest waning perceptibly." What causes this? Not the "thunderous denunciations by some preacher," said Matthews. Nor did it come about because of aggressive demands to give up "such carnal pursuits." Rather, wrote Matthews from his observations, what happened "was the undemonstrative voice of the Holy Spirit influencing daily conduct, turning thought into new channels, producing the instantaneous results that no other power could have accomplished."[9]

4. Revival Would Cut the Divorce Rate

Sangster lamented the climb in Britain's divorce rate from 1,385 divorces in 1876–1880 to almost 150,000 in the 1950s. He spoke of statistics all too evident in our own time that reveal the negative impact on children, juvenile delinquency, and poverty. However, he said, true revival would transform the situation. "Sound religion gives us new homes," he wrote.

That's what happened when revival swept into homes and families in Wales fifty-three years earlier. For example, a young man came into one of the revival meetings, and people could tell he was in serious distress. He cupped his face in his hands as he bent forward. The man was godless and had tormented his family with his cruelty. Individuals began to pray with and counsel him. Finally he declared he was going to walk a new course with a new life. Meanwhile, an elderly blind man entered the chapel and sat down across the room. The old man was the father of the young man in distress. Another man eased into the pew and sat beside the blind man. He was the father-in-law of the man who was in agony of heart. The father and the father-in-law were astonished "and rejoicing that such a character should be changed."[10]

The next day the young man went to his wife and asked her to forgive him. Then he sought out his brother, from whom he had been alienated, and asked his forgiveness. That night the man who had been so cruel was back in the revival service. He was impressed five or six times to lift his arm and praise God, and every time he did, someone stood and confessed Christ as their Savior. Later he said that "the Spirit of God kept telling me to pray for someone else, then signified that my prayer was heard, and so I lifted my arm and praised Him."[11]

5. Revival Would Reduce Juvenile Crime

"The adolescent thug is a feature of our generation," Sangster wrote. "What is the answer to this appalling problem?" he asked. "The police struggle gallantly against it," as do the courts who "seek to be firm without being savage," and all the while "Parliament is perplexed." Then Sangster observed the need for "a new tide of religion in our national life" because, among other things, "it is exceedingly rare for a young criminal to be associated with church or Sunday school *at the time his crimes are committed*" (italics added).

Sangster doubtless could recall that a half-century earlier, the Welsh Revival had been primarily a youth movement. When Evan Roberts left school at Newscastle to return to Loughor and Moriah Chapel to seek God for revival, he began by organizing the young people there to intercede. It wasn't just the youth already in the church who were impacted but outsiders, like a young coal miner who came home for Christmas from the pits of Glamorganshire. Usually the coal miner and his friends would spend much of the holiday time in pubs, getting drunk, and creating havoc everywhere they went. But his first night at home on Christmas 1904 "was not spent in the village inn, but in the village chapel," wrote H. Elvet Lewis. The turnaround in his life surprised the little community. "Such a ring-leader of drink and dissipation could not have been so suddenly changed!"[12]

He was transformed by the influence of Jesus Christ invading his life through dynamic revival. The old life could not withstand the invasion and was pushed out by the strength of the Holy Spirit.

6. *Revival Would Lessen the Prison Population*

"Is it only a coincidence that the generation which saw the churches empty saw the prisons full?" Sangster asked. "The exhaustion of Britain's moral capital is more serious in some ways than the exhaustion of her monetary capital." Decency, he continued, "needs support, a buttress, something to hold it up and give authority," and such undergirding strength is ministered in authentic revival.

As we saw in a previous chapter, as the Welsh Revival progressed into 1905, judges in the areas impacted by spiritual awakening began to wear white gloves at the bench, signifying there were no cases on their dockets. The *South Wales Daily News* covered the revival and reported: "Infidels were converted; drunkards, thieves, and gamblers saved, and many reclaimed to respectability and honored citizenship. . . . Several police courts had clean sheets and were idle."[13]

7. *Revival Would Improve the Quality and Increase the Output of Work*

In 1957, in light of a sagging economy, Sangster asked raw pragmatic questions: "How can you make a man work who doesn't want to? How can you prevent a loafer living a parasitic life on the Welfare State and twisting noble legislation to ignoble ends?"

The same questions confront the twenty-first century. No doubt many of the domestic policy makers in 1964 had noble intentions for the Great Society legislation that expanded the welfare state in America. But in addition to the good it accomplished, it also created a culture of dependence and entitlement.

"Real religion makes a radical difference to daily work," Sangster pointed out, because a person awakens to the reality that he or she is working for God's glory. "It must be done well; it is *for God*" (italics in original).

The Welsh Revival demonstrated the proof of that claim. Strikes had impacted morale, output, and earnings in the Welsh industries, not only in the mines but in the quarries. Revival lightning struck at Llanfairfechan and nearby Bethesda in 1904, and the mine managers reported their workers had become better miners.[14]

A local newspaper reported that "the results [of the revival] have been most gratifying, especially in the healing of old quarrels and feuds which have been caused by the Penrhyn strike." Though the strike had stopped at the quarry, it had produced "disastrous results" that were "apparent in the social and religious relations of the neighbourhood." Yet, the newspaper reported, "a week's revival services have done more to heal the breach than years of effort by ordinary methods."[15]

A reporter for the *Western Mail* accompanied a group of miners as they were beginning the night shift. They went down a half hour before the shift began so they could have a prayer meeting without interrupting work. "Seventy yards from the bottom of the shaft, in the stables, we came to the prayer meeting," the correspondent related. A miner was reading from the gospel of Matthew while miners' lamps bathed the scene in light. The workers grouped around him. "Earnest men, all of them," said the reporter. "Faces that bore the scars of the underground toiler; downcast eyes that seemed to be 'the homes of silent prayer'; strong frames that quivered with a new emotion."[16]

A worker came into conflict with his boss and threatened to stir up unrest at one of the mines, feeling he had been wrongly accused regarding the quality of his work. The man was determined to go to a union committee with a proposal for action against management. But he went first to a revival meeting conducted by Evan Roberts. Evan preached about the impact of the Holy Spirit on the human heart. The worker realized his intent to disrupt work in the mine would not be proper. He went back to the mine managers, promised not to provoke action, and asked if he could go back to work. Permission was granted and the issue was settled peacefully while also addressing the abuse and preventing anyone from losing an income because of a strike.[17]

8. Revival Would Restore to the Nation a Sense of High Destiny

There was a time when the British were united in the belief that their nation "had a special and high destiny in the world," wrote Sangster. "Some aspects of the idea were a little silly," he noted, because there was the tendency by some national leaders to conflate the British Empire with the kingdom of God. Old memorial tablets celebrating great military leaders and their exploits that hung on the walls of some churches seemed to imply "that whoever resisted British arms resisted heaven."[18]

But Sangster felt that the British people had lost any sense of destiny. She still had good things to give to the world. "The doctrine of the essential superiority of one race over another is false," he said, and "the only kingdom with a future is the Kingdom of God." However, Britain "has a longer history and experience of self-government than any other large nation on the face of the globe," he maintained.

How are the smug and cruel presumptions of national destiny, as seen, for example, in Nazi Germany, shoved out of the soul of a nation? How does one displace reckless militarism and chauvinism with a servant heart? The answer, as we have seen, is the kingdom of God, the realm of righteousness (justice), peace, and Spirit-given joy (Rom. 14:17). But how does the kingdom of God become manifest in a nation?

Jesus, as we noted in an earlier chapter, did not give the keys of kingdom authority to civil government but to the true church. Authority in the civil sphere is thus derived, not seized. When the church experiences revival, there can be displacement in the society of all that makes a nation a danger rather than a blessing to the world.

"One of the most astonishing incidents" of the Welsh Revival occurred in January 1905 at Pwllhelli, said Eifion Evans. Supporters of David Lloyd George, at that time a local member of Parliament, were holding a political rally that "naturally and irresistibly" turned into "a religious service." Lloyd George himself was caught up in the spirit of spiritual awakening. Before the outbreak of the revival in 1904, Lloyd George had spoken of the principality's great need. "The material conditions of this country will not improve until there comes a spiritual awakening," he said, and he encouraged pastors to promote and foster "such a revival."

When the revival came, Lloyd George said it was like a great wind surging over the principality, with, in Eifion Evans's recounting, "far-reaching national and social changes."[19] Just how far-reaching the changes were was evident slightly more than a decade later, when Lloyd George became prime minister of Britain. The experience of the revival years earlier was still alive in his spirit and soul, the prime minister said.

9. Revival Would Make Us Invincible in Any War of Ideas

Sangster wrote amid Cold War tensions that emerged after the Second World War. The "war of ideas" in his era was between the Western Judeo-Christian worldview and Marxist socialism and official state atheism.

"What is at war in the war of ideas?" Sangster asked. His answer began with what he considered the core of the war of ideas: "Is God there or is He not? Is man His child with a life after death—or just what he eats? Is the last explanation of the universe spiritual or material?"[20]

In our age a war is raging between the Judeo-Christian worldview and progressivism, which is actually a secular attempt to achieve the fruits of revival. Secular progressivism, as our times show, takes on the worst forms of pharisaic religious zeal. The inquisitions continue, not in some Spanish torture chamber, but in the academies and institutions under the control of the secular religion. The wooden stocks are gone from town squares, but the stocks are still in the public square, putting on display for the sake of ridicule and intimidation any who depart from the doctrine of the religion of progressivism.

All the issues dear to today's progressives were addressed powerfully and effectively in the Welsh Revival. For example, there was hardly any consciousness of sexism, as seen in the prominent role of women in the revival. We noted above the impact of the revival on the workplace and the improvement of economic well-being. We have seen the revival's context of social equality—its major leaders were common folk, with its most noted a young man from the mines and the smithy's forge.

These attributes came not from regulation or other attempts to force equality or to set quotas. The revival's character was formed without the inquisitors who wielded whips and terrorized those who had departed from the faith. Instead, there was the Holy Spirit, wooing sinners to receive the love of the Father and sparking renewal everywhere, from the bottom of the coal pit to the estates of the mine owners.

10. Revival Would Give Happiness and Peace to the People

In his day, Sangster noted the "only hope of happiness which millions entertain is to win something big on the [gambling] pools."[21] In our time, winning a national lottery is the happiness quest of multitudes. Sangster also lamented the evidences of the lack of peace in his time. Uncertainties about the future plagued many.

But, wrote Sangster, the only place one can find peace is deep in the hearts of people who know God. The peace and joy they experience "does not depend on circumstances" but upon "conviction and communion." Peace, he said, must be received from God.

Scores of people discovered the distinct style of joy and peace in the Welsh Revival was unique because the conviction of sin, which one would think would rob a person of joy and peace, was at the same time an experience that brought both. This meant the joy and peace were not facades overlaying a rotten core. One of the indications of the happiness and peace ministered through the revival was reflected in statistics related to alcohol abuse. In 1903, there were 10,528 convictions for drunkenness in Glanmorgan, but in 1906, in the wake of the revival there, that number dropped to 5,490. One commentator said, "Three months of the revival had done more to sober the country than the temperance effort of many years."[22]

The revival's manifestation of joy and peace was authentic, exposing all, and yet immersed in delight of spirit and soul that made its way to the body. "When our soul came to taste the feasts of Heaven, the flesh also insisted on having its share, and all the passions of nature aroused by grace were rioting tumultuously," said William Williams of Pantycelyn.[23]

This was not cheap happiness or counterfeit peace, but true joy and authentic peace. Rev. J. T. Job, a pastor in Bethesda, Caernarfonshire, described the curious combination of conviction, joy, and peace he experienced during a revival meeting:

One thing I know: *"Thursday night, December the 22nd, 1904"* will be inscribed in letters of fire in my heart forever! . . . I felt the *Holy Spirit* like a torrent of light causing my whole nature to shake; I saw *Jesus Christ*—and my nature melted at His feet; I saw *myself*—until I abhorred it! And what more can I say? . . . O! the Love of God in the Death of the Cross is exceedingly powerful![24]

Usually when people think of spiritual warfare, what comes to mind is *The Exorcist* or harrowing accounts of hysterical demonized people shrieking, gnawing, or throwing themselves on the floor as someone ministers deliverance—and those things do happen. But as we have stated, all deliverance ultimately is the displacement of the powers of darkness by the sheer weight of the authority of God's kingdom manifested in true spiritual awakening, of which the Welsh Revival is an example.

The very weight that brings about the displacement of the principalities and powers rests heavily on the finite human beings who minister the power of Jesus Christ and His kingdom, sometimes with phenomena that seem strange and hard to understand.

This is what happened to Evan Roberts.

CHAPTER 13

The Weight of God's Glory

*To carry the weight that comes with leading
a revival, especially for a nation, all three
parts of the human being—spirit, soul,
and body—must be made strong.*

—ROBERTS LIARDON[1]

As the revival advanced both in time and space, more attention was focused upon Evan Roberts. Increasingly, the revival was identified in the public mind with him and he with the revival.

With the spreading awareness of Evan and the revival—and even fame—there were those who seemed to wonder if he was a manifestation of the demonic disguised as an "angel of light" (2 Cor. 11:14) or, more generously, merely a man who had lost his mind.

Evan, wrote Brynmor Pierce Jones, "came under personal attack as a lunatic at worst and eccentric at best," but Evan "did not help matters." Jones had in mind Evan's actions that "worried his fellow workers," like "jumping to his feet in the middle of a meeting and accusing the people of not being earnest."[2]

J. Vynrwy Morgan and Peter Price were especially intense in their criticisms of Evan. Neither was opposed to revival—they both knew the spiritual history of their land—but they greatly disliked the man hailed as the leader of the revival of 1904–5.

In 1906, Morgan wrote a critique of the revival—*The Welsh Religious Revival, 1904–5: A Retrospect and a Criticism*—which disturbed F. B. Meyer so much that he wrote Morgan a letter expressing the hope "that nothing of adverse criticism of the past may affect either him [Roberts] or the work of God through him."[3] Nevertheless, Morgan noted there were people of "unquestioned and unquestionable" piety who were excited initially about the revival, but "to their natures Evan Roberts did not, and possibly could not, appeal." Such godly people, Morgan suggested, "looked for the image and superscription of the heaven-sent messenger, and were disappointed."[4]

Peter Price found even more to disdain in Evan Roberts. Price had graduated in 1901 from Cambridge and by 1904 was pastor of Bethania Chapel in Dowlais. After Evan visited Bethania, Price was so disturbed that he penned a letter to the *Western Mail* that created a stir. The paper itself saw the letter as so notorious that it was newsworthy. On February 4, 1905, a correspondent wrote:

> The religious public in this country were shocked this week by the publication in the "Western Mail" of a letter by the Rev. Peter Price, a Dowlais pastor, in which that gentleman made a most unjustifiable attack upon Mr. Evan Roberts and the Revival, with which he is so closely associated and in the progress of which he is universally acknowledged to be the chief human factor.

Journalist E. Morgan Humphreys initially shared Price's and Morgan's views, but as he observed Evan and the revival, Humphreys's opinion changed "radically." Humphreys wrote:

> The more I saw of him, the deeper my love for him and my respect for him became. It was impossible not to respect his mental ability; some of his addresses were brilliant; they did not contain a trace of superficial appeal to sentiment, and it is a great mistake to presume that Evan Roberts was a religious spell-binder. . . . It was unfortunate for him that many people were afraid of him. . . . He was completely natural, he was jovial in company and at the same time he possessed a simple and wholly natural dignity which made it impossible for anyone to take advantage of him. . . . He did not make any appeal to the emotions. . . . It would not be far off the mark were I to say that his appeal was almost invariably to the mind and the conscience. . . . Whatever my ideas are about the Revival—those are mixed—I have only one opinion of Evan Roberts.[5]

WHAT TO MAKE OF IT ALL

What, then, do we make of this? Was Peter Price writing from his own petulance or did he discern an alien spirit at work in Evan Roberts? Did J. Vynrwy Morgan spot some subtly dangerous doctrinal aberration in Evan and his message or was he simply jealous at the fame accorded a nobody like Roberts?

On the other hand, what of Roberts's many supporters—like E. Morgan Humphreys—who, through direct observation, interaction, and relationship with Evan, deemed him a chosen vessel of God?

Decades later, Lewis Drummond, another scholar focusing on theology and revival, had a more balanced and insightful view than Morgan or Price. Drummond, whom I knew personally, was a consultant and workshop leader for the Billy Graham Evangelistic Association and came to occupy the Billy Graham Chair of Evangelism at Southern Baptist Theological Seminary in addition to teaching at Spurgeon's College, London. Drummond studied and wrote extensively on the revivals that had occurred across the centuries and around the world, including the Welsh Revival. He observed that a revival leader

> is normally called upon to pay a high price. The drain and strain can be tremendous. In John Wesley's journal we read, "March 17, 1752. At the Foundry. How pleasing it would be to flesh and blood to remain at this little quiet place, where at length to weather this storm! Nay, I am not to consult my own ease but the advancing of the Kingdom of God." Evan Roberts, the prophet of the Welsh Revival, was so shattered by the work that he was never able to preach again. . . . Savonarola was burned at the stake. That was his price to pay.[6]

My own conclusion after extensive research and reflection on Evan Roberts and the Welsh Revival is that Evan was a man with a heavy anointing of the Holy Spirit for the ministry of the revival. Human flesh is limited by its finitude in its capacity to bear this weight of anointing. The body and soul grow weary under this great empowerment, even while the Spirit-indwelt human spirit continues to pulsate with its energy. Out of that weariness the flesh can shove aside the spirit, and the spiritual leader's fallen humanity is exposed.

This is not, as Jesse Penn-Lewis and Evan himself tried to argue in their book, *War on the Saints*,[7] a takeover by the powers of darkness. It is rather godly people coming to the point of mental, emotional, and physical exhaustion. Certainly, such a condition can give ground to demonic influence, but that should not be the default judgment (as it seems to be in *War on the Saints*) when a leader whose life and ministry have consistently manifested the work of God suddenly—or gradually—speaks and behaves in a shocking manner not worthy of himself or herself.

Yes, we are to be alert lest we give the demons a foothold within us, but we should also face honestly the limitations of our frail humanity and know when to pull aside for a period of rest. Brynmor Pierce Jones, a Roberts biographer who respected him and his work, understood the importance of those under an intense and remarkable anointing being alert for the devil who "prowls around like a roaring lion, seeking someone to devour" (1 Peter 5:8).

"How such a modest, self-effacing man, so keen to be out of sight, could gradually, in his public ministry, turn into a very directive person, is not just a riddle for psychologists to solve. It should be accepted as a solemn warning to all those who are called to such special ministries in our day and generation," Jones concluded.[8]

LIMITATIONS OF HUMAN FLESH

As the apostle Paul wrote, "We have this treasure in earthen vessels" (2 Cor. 4:7). In a person like Evan Roberts, in whom both the fruit and gifts of the Spirit are so evident, what critics saw as evidences of the bizarre must be analyzed in the context of the Holy Spirit's anointing of the individual. In short, Evan was neither demonized nor deranged but dynamized to bear an intense bolt of lightning that would burn him out—as well as any human with a kingdom mission as heavy as that given to him.

If this seems a heretical or offensive view, there are ample biblical and historical verifications. Paul wrote to the Galatians that we are not to "lose heart in doing good" and that "in due time we will reap if we do not grow weary" (6:9). The anointing of the Holy Spirit is heavy with intensity, and human beings on whom this empowerment rests must not succumb to either the hubris of thinking they can ignore the signs of exhaustion or the false humility of boasting about how they must work nonstop because the work all depends on them.

Edwin Orr, a scholar and historian of revival, noted there were reports in March 1905 that Evan's health was declining. "The strain of incessant travel, irregular meals, and long hours in meetings, added their quota to the toll on his health," Orr observed.[9] At the same time, as an examination by physicians in Liverpool showed, he was sane and mentally stable.

If Evan was deficient in anything, it may have been in recognizing the intensity of the Holy Spirit's anointing upon him and exercising stewardship of that empowerment by going aside—as Jesus Himself did—to commune with the Lord and recover physical strength.

There were contemporaries of Evan Roberts and the revival who were every bit as credentialed and respected as J. Vynrwy Morgan and Peter Price who understood Evan and his extremes as well as his solid leadership in the context of the weight of glory thrust upon him through the anointing of the Holy Spirit. They saw Evan, first, as an impassioned intercessor for revival and, second, as the key human instrument—among many—who would draw the bolt of the 1904–5 revival.

These people who best understood Evan in the context of anointing included H. Elvet Lewis, who described the kinds of stresses that were on Evan, referring to a particularly busy time.

Lewis wrote that the strain "must have been intense, physically and spiritually. He went on, day by day, through thronging multitudes, alternating from grief to rapture, often within a few brief hours."[10]

R. A. Torrey was one of the most noted evangelists of the late nineteenth and early twentieth centuries. He was an American and closely associated with Dwight L. Moody. Torrey also was known in Britain and other countries. Perhaps more than most others, Torrey could understand the weight resting on Evan Roberts and wrote to him:

> I am praying that God will keep you simply trusting in Him and obedient to Him, going not where men shall call you but going where He shall lead you, and that He may keep you humble. It is so easy for us to become exalted when God uses us as the instruments of His power. It is so easy to think that we are something ourselves. When we get to thinking that, God will set us aside. . . . May God keep you humble, and fill you more and more with His mighty power. I hope that someday I may have the privilege of meeting you.[11]

The Filling and the Baptism

The work of the Holy Spirit is the mighty power that manifests the weight of God's glory in and through human beings. To understand Roberts and his style, actions, and behaviors, we must look more closely at two functions of the Holy Spirit in the lives of people who've given themselves to Jesus Christ and the service of His kingdom: the filling with the Holy Spirit and the baptism with the Holy Spirit.

Being filled with the Holy Spirit is empowerment for a Christlike lifestyle.

The baptism with the Spirit is the anointing that comes upon persons alive in Christ to empower them to do the works of God in line with their calling and through their spiritual gifts.

One way to understand Evan Roberts—and any Christ-saved, Spirit-filled, baptized believer that God might anoint to lead an end-times revival—is to note the linkage between calling, gifts, and personality. Every woman or man in Christ has a calling in ministering the kingdom of God in the world. The gifts of the Spirit are the ministry abilities of Jesus Christ distributed at Pentecost across the body of Christ—the church. Jesus told His disciples that they would do the same works that He did (see John 14:12). The gifts made and continue to make it possible for the true church to continue His incarnate ministry in the world. Only Jesus Christ of Nazareth ministered the totality of the gifts. His people are given those gifts necessary to implement their calling and ministry in the world.

The gifts give shape to personality. A study of Evan Roberts's passion and the ministry through which he expressed it gives us a hint of his spiritual gifts. Certainly he was an evangelist whose primary concern to see revival was that at least one hundred thousand people would be converted to Christ. He probably had a gift of mercy, as his weeping for the salvation of his people showed. There was something of the prophetic in him as well. Occasionally he moved in the gift of knowledge, which some interpreted as clairvoyance.

What kind of personality would these gifts form? Such a person must have a high level of sensitivity along with a driving need to get the work done. The prophetic, under the dominance of flesh, can be overbearing. Mercy will sometimes deteriorate into emotionalism. Evangelism, influenced by the flesh, can become manipulative.

Queen Elizabeth told an interviewer about the difficulty of wearing the crown of the British monarchy. "You can't look down to read the speech," she said, and so "you have to take the speech [manuscript] up." Otherwise, "your neck would break" and the crown "would fall off."[12]

The weightiness of the Holy Spirit's anointing might not break the neck of the one on whom it rests, but its heaviness is in the passion it stimulates and the power that flows through the person as he or she ministers. A woman desperate for Jesus' touch of healing struggled through a crowd, touched the edge of the hem of His robe, and was healed immediately.

"Who is the one who touched Me?" asked Jesus, quickly.

"Master, the people are crowding and pressing in on You," Peter replied.

"Someone did touch Me," Jesus answered, "*for I was aware that power had gone out of Me*" (see Luke 8:43–48, italics added).

There are two types of anointing given at Pentecost—the *corporate* anointing upon the body of Christ universally and the *personal* anointing for every individual or "member" of the body, tied to her or his specific calling, ministry, and mission. Every believer shares in the corporate anointing released upon the body of Christ when he or she is baptized into Christ's church. The apostle John wrote, "The anointing you received from him remains in you" (1 John 2:27 NIV).

This means the corporate anointing is *ontological*, that is, it is the spiritual energy and drive at the core of our very being as people in whom the Holy Spirit dwells. And it does not go away.

The personal anointing is *functional* and *missional*. It is the *exousia* (authority granting the right to minister God's will and purpose) and *dunamis* (power to actualize and produce the effects of the ministry).

The corporate anointing is continual, never going away, and every person in Christ and indwelt by the Holy Spirit is under that weighty crown. The personal anointing is linked directly to a specific ministry calling and need, and it may lift as the work is completed, to be followed by a fresh anointing as we embark on a new ministry assignment in the kingdom. Thus, while the corporate anointing is *continual*, the personal anointing is *situational*.

Luke tells of a day when Jesus was teaching a crowd, "and the power of the Lord was present for Him to perform healing" (5:17). On another day in Nazareth, Jesus "did not do many miracles there because of their unbelief" (Matt. 13:58).

EFFECTS OF ANOINTING

Evan Roberts did indeed perform actions that some considered extreme, bizarre, inappropriate, and ill-timed. No doubt the leader of the coming global outpouring will do the same. Yet there were many, even in Evan's time, when the criticisms were intense and actions sometime bewildering, who saw him through the eyes of the spirit, and in the context of his anointing.

Rev. Thomas Phillips noted Evan's great burden for the lost. With regard to the weight of anointing upon Evan, Phillips wrote:

A type of suffering arises from sympathy with the redeeming purpose of Christ. To watch with Him and work for His Kingdom is to be hurt by everything that hurts Him. To follow Him is to take up the Cross. Our Cross is like His in so far as it is caused by sins and endured in order to help others live.[13]

Those who would rush to judgment, thinking Evan confused, overwrought, or extreme, might not note that other revivalists had similar experiences. David Morgan, a major leader in the 1859 revival, had a comparable story.

Eifion Evans described this as happening just before Morgan launched out in the work of revival. Morgan, he said, had "not yet received power from on high" as he rushed home to a prayer meeting. But suddenly Morgan's "bosom was agitated by intense and conflicting emotions." He realized that the blessing he had sought for years was "at hand, awaiting his acceptance." He went to bed and to sleep as usual, but he was awakened at 4:00 a.m., "instantly conscious that some strange, mysterious change had come over him." He was awestruck at "the marvelous illumination of his faculties," and later said, "I awoke about four in the morning remembering everything of a religious nature that I had ever learnt or heard."[14]

Something similar also happened to Welsh reformer Howell Harris almost a century before, when revival lightning struck Wales. Harris wrote in his diary on July 18, 1775, that while he was in "secret prayer," he "felt suddenly my heart melting within me, like wax before the fire, with love to God my Saviour. . . . There was in me 'a well of water springing up into everlasting life'; yea, 'the love of God was shed abroad in my heart by the Holy Ghost' [John 4:14; Rom. 5:5]."

Eifion Evans, according to D. Martyn Lloyd-Jones, was a uniquely qualified scholar as both a historian and theologian. In his writings about Evan Roberts, Evans sought to understand both the spiritual and psychological dynamics of the man and his ministry. Evans recognized the heaviness of God's anointing upon Roberts and the effects, and he wrote of Roberts's "sheer anguish of soul."[15]

Evans attributed Roberts's despondency to "the Church's impotence to reach the unconverted."[16] Evans also reported the interview between Roberts and newspaper editor W. T. Stead, when Roberts described how, at the beginning of his revival ministry "the pressure became greater and greater" to go back to the schoolroom in Loughor to speak to the young people there who would form the core of his initial work of the revival.[17]

The weighty anointing upon Evan Roberts and others in the revival settled upon people who had come from other nations to see and learn from what was happening in Wales. They, too, began to feel the intensity for their own societies. David Matthews wrote of a night when the anointing fell on an audience as Evan was preaching: "Several voices, representing different countries, were heard interceding for their beloved homeland."

First, there was China, then a Baptist pastor from Russia "wept as he confessed the sins of the nation as Daniel did centuries ago." With a heart broken for his country, a pastor from Germany prayed, comparing "the greatness of days gone by, when Luther shook the world, with his own day when his fellow countrymen were following the vain philosophies of men."

The French region of Brittany "had a voice speaking to the Lord in broken Welsh." The intercessor "cried to the Lord for ungodly France and for his friends enduring persecution there."

A Japanese prayer warrior waited patiently for the "fiery Welsh enthusiasm" to abate, and then, in a gulf of silence, "brought Japan before the Lord in a very definite way."

In the same room were Russians, whose country was at war with Japan, yet "the representatives of both nations" were "at perfect peace with one another, worshipping in an atmosphere that was pregnant with great possibilities for both peoples." In fact, "there was not the slightest evidence of enmity visible between these men; both were praying for revival."

Newspapers picked up on the story: "Russia and Japan at war in the East! Russia and Japan at peace in the West, in a small Welsh chapel!"[18]

From that small Welsh chapel in that small British principality, the revival spread to many parts of the world. And even today it sparks our vision and strengthens our faith in anticipation of the great end-times revival that will precede the day the weight of God's glory will rest upon all the nations, suffocating enmity, snuffing out gunfire, squelching the power of bombs, stifling factions, and silencing hell.

There would be previews of that glorious day as the weighty revival anointing spread from Wales across the world.

CHAPTER 14

The Reach of the Revival

*I believe the world is upon the threshold of a great
religious revival, and I pray that I may be allowed to help
bring this about. I beseech all those who confess Christ
to ask Him today, upon their knees, if He has not some
work for them to do now. He will lead them all as He
has led us. He will make them pillars of smoke by day
and pillars of fire by night to guide all men to Him.*

—Evan Roberts[1]

Had you been alive in 1907 and visiting Pyongyang in Korea,
you might have strolled the streets in awe at the number of
church steeples. Now seat of the communist Kim tyranny and religious cult, where streets thunder periodically with military parades,
the metropolis was once called the "Jerusalem of the East." The
thriving Christian community there in the early twentieth century
was due to the impact of the Welsh Revival on Korea.

Revival lightning struck Korea on January 6–7, 1907. What has come to be called the "Korean Pentecost" was sparked as missionaries gathered for weeks of prayer. Word of the Welsh Revival made it across the globe to the Korean Peninsula's northern territory, and revival exploded across the region.[2] While there were periods of decline, revival's impact and fruit continued to be manifest in Korea even during the Second World War. Despite persecution by Japanese occupying forces, there were three times more Christians in northern Korea than in southern Korea, according to Jin-Heon Jung.[3]

Korea, as we will see, was not the only place to be influenced by the Welsh Revival. Revival historian J. Edwin Orr pointed out that all the inhabited continents experienced some level of "a noticeable and spontaneous spiritual awakening around 1905." All, he said, to some degree had been impacted by the Welsh Revival that began in 1904.[4]

"The present worldwide revival was rocked in the little cradle of Wales," said Frank Bartleman, who played a major role in the early twentieth-century Azusa Street Revival that many credit with launching the modern pentecostal movement. H. Elvet described it like this:

> It is as when a farmer, one autumn afternoon, turns out to set the hillside gorse on fire. He lights a small bush, and perhaps it fails. He lights it again, then another, and there is a local blaze. He passes on to another part and does the same, and there are several red patches of fire. Then a servant, quick and eager, takes a dry, uprooted bush, just fringing with flame, and he runs along, leaving a line of fire building at a score of points, flame meets flame, fire kindles fire, sparks are caught in the wind and sow new flame on every hand . . . Evan Roberts

became the herald of that fire, he helped to join together the separate patches of fire; the whole was caught in the great wind of God, and before 1904 passed away, the greater part of Wales was in a fervor of prayer and song . . . By the end of January (1905) I could discover no town or hamlet, or sequestered mountain spot, but the divine fire was there."[5]

No Surprise

The spread of revival should not be a surprise. And it won't be during the coming end-times revival. The inherent nature of the kingdom of God, of which Spirit-given revival is a manifestation, is expansion, advance, and progress. Jesus' parables of the kingdom show that once the kingdom seed is sown into the good soil, growth and spread are inevitable. Or to return to H. Elvet Lewis's analogy, once the gorse (a shrub that bursts out in yellow blooms) catches fire, its very nature is to leap across the landscape.

Jesus began a series of kingdom parables in Matthew 13 by talking about a sower, the seed, and the quality of the soil. We have previously discussed the importance of the ground in calling down and receiving the lightning of revival, but here Jesus uses the metaphor of planting seed. Again the ground—in the form of the soil—is crucial. The seed that fell on the good soil, said Jesus, "yielded a crop, some a hundredfold, some sixty, and some thirty" (v. 8). The yield comes from the spread of the roots that spring from the seed. True revival will be marked by spread and fruit, while human-contrived events labeled as revival will produce blooms that will not endure, along with roots that will quickly wither and die.

Also in the Matthew 13 discourse the Lord illustrates the nature of His kingdom by comparing it to a mustard seed:

The kingdom of heaven is like a mustard seed, which a man took and sowed in his field; and this is smaller than all other seeds, but when it is full grown, it is larger than the garden plants and becomes a tree, so that THE BIRDS OF THE AIR come and NEST IN ITS BRANCHES. (vv. 31–32)

Again the emphasis is on growth and spread. The advance of the root system springing from the miniscule seed leads to a tree so expansive that many living things find sanctuary in its branches. So the spread of the Welsh Revival—as it will be with the coming end-times revival—was characterized by multitudes of people across the world nesting in its many branches, encompassing many cultures, languages, and social groups.

As I write these words, my mind goes to a ten-day period in 1969 in New York City. I was covering a Billy Graham Crusade in Madison Square Garden. I also assisted the Graham team as a volunteer, helping to counsel new believers and helping to coordinate media relations.

While one cannot always equate true revival with human-organized campaigns, this does not mean that the Spirit of the Lord does not come upon human events at times with revival anointing. The Holy Spirit was indeed sending revival lightning on that crusade.

Outside the crusade venue, the streets of New York thundered with the chaos of protest, violence, rioting, and dangerous disorder. But inside Madison Square Garden was a sanctuary of peace and hope. Standing just below and beside the platform from which Billy Graham spoke night after night, I scanned the crowd. I was amazed at the diversity. It seemed every continent, if not every nation, was represented, along with every race and every economic group. The choir behind the platform was a microcosm of the vast audience.

People had gathered in that arena and found respite and sanctuary as praise was lifted to heaven and Billy Graham proclaimed Jesus Christ and His salvation. Decades later, when I think of the mustard seed and the great tree that sprang from it, I cannot help but think about the panorama I scanned night after night when Madison Square Garden was a hall of peace and hope for the multitudes.

Jesus' parable of the leaven is particularly illustrative of the nature of kingdom advance and the revivals that are its expressions, along with their continuing impact: "The kingdom of heaven is like leaven, which a woman took and hid in three pecks of flour until it was all leavened" (Matt. 13:33).

There are three dynamics of the manifestation of the kingdom that will also characterize the end-times revival revealed in this short parable:

Penetration

Leaven is a piece of dough that is pulled out of the mass and set apart to undergo fermentation. This results in the transformation of the original pinch that has been taken from the lump. When the transformative work is complete, the leaven is embedded back into the batch.

This is a striking illustration of the nature of the remnant community: the church. It is the *ekklesia*—the people who are called out of the world. But the church is not pulled out of the world to live in isolation from the world. This community undergoes the transformative work of sanctification so it can impart a new quality of life into the world.

As the crucial hour of the cross and atonement neared, Jesus prayed both for His disciples at that time and those who will follow Him across history:

I have given them Your word; and the world has hated them, because they are not of the world, even as I am not of the world. I do not ask You to take them out of the world, but to keep them from the evil one. They are not of the world, even as I am not of the world. Sanctify them in the truth; Your word is truth. As You sent Me into the world, I also have sent them into the world. For their sakes I sanctify Myself, that they themselves also may be sanctified in truth. (John 17:14–19)

The point of Jesus' remnant people being separated from the world is not that they may live blissfully apart from the world and its miseries. The purpose of being set apart (sanctified) is to undergo a process of personal growth in the Spirit (sanctification) for the sake of *being put back into the world, to penetrate it with the gospel of the kingdom* (see Matt. 24:14).

This is in view when the apostle Peter wrote of the church, "You are A CHOSEN RACE, a royal PRIESTHOOD, A HOLY NATION, A PEOPLE FOR God's OWN POSSESSION, so that you may proclaim the excellencies of Him who has called you out of darkness into His marvelous light" (1 Peter 2:9).

The church's mission leading up to the coming end-times revival will be—as it always has been—the proclamation of Christ and His kingdom, which is intensified and advanced in the world in and through authentic revival.

Pervasion

Jesus said that the leaven was hidden in "three pecks of flour until it was all leavened" (Matt. 13:33).

The whole purpose of history, Jesus said, is to provide the arena for the advance of the gospel of the kingdom, the core message of true revival, so that it can be proclaimed in *all* the world as a witness to all the nations (*ethne*, "peoples" or "ethnicities") and then the "end" (*telos*, "purpose" and "goal") will come (see Matt. 24:14).

Therefore, permeation of the message of the kingdom into all spheres in preparation for the end-times revival is inevitable when the Spirit of God moves across the world through His set-apart people like He is today. Jesus tells His followers to go into all the world on the basis of His authority to make disciples of all *ethnes*, to baptize them in the name of the Father, Son, and Holy Spirit and to instruct them in everything He has commanded His disciples (see Matt. 28:18–20).

At the moment of His ascension, Jesus told His bedazzled followers that once the Holy Spirit comes upon them, they are to start where they are, in Jerusalem, then spread into Judea, the larger area in which Jerusalem is situated, then into the region, by taking the gospel of the kingdom into Samaria and ultimately to "the remotest part of the earth" (Acts 1:7–8).

As this happens, we see that Jesus was not speaking merely of the *geographical* spread of the gospel but its permeation into all spheres of human endeavor: the family, education, governance, business and the marketplace, the arts and media. Paul sowed the gospel of the kingdom in the geopolitical entity known as Greece but also into the soil of the Athenian philosophers. He also proclaimed the message of Christ and His kingdom in Rome through his witness and that of others among the Jesus followers in Rome and into the very household of Caesar.

Precipitation

The leaven is catalytic because it has been transformed. It brings its own new nature into contact with the world and precipitates transformation in everything it touches.

We see this powerfully revealed in the Welsh Revival and in others we cite in this chapter as it will be in the true move of God at the end of history. The coming end-times revival will be cata-lytic, transforming people and even societies into Christlikeness. If a revival is not catalytic, it is not revival.

This does not mean mere utilitarian progressivism. All move-ments in the fallen world, as we will see in the next chapter, will undergo entropy—the pull of fallenness into disorder, decay, death, and disintegration. This is why revival is often described as *renewal*. God will move anew and afresh in every epoch until the greatest of revivals will come at the Lord's appearing again in the world. At that point there will be no need for people to instruct others to "know the LORD" because "they will all know Me, from the least of them to the greatest of them" (Jer. 31:31–34; see also Heb. 8:7–12).

When that occurs, "re" will disappear in the word *revival* because the "vivication" will be permanent, impermeable to any outside influences that might try to drag the new world and the new life within it to a lower quality. At that time, the gospel of the kingdom and its transforming work will have spread into the totality of the world. The earth will be filled with the glory of God (see Isa. 6:3), the knowledge of the glory of God (see Hab. 2:14), and the praise of God (see Hab. 3:3), because "EVERY KNEE WILL BOW . . . and . . . every tongue will confess that Jesus Christ is Lord, to the glory of God the Father" (Phil. 2:10–11).

Until then, we continue doing the work of the kingdom in antici-pation of that glorious day when God will send down the lightning that will ignite the final end-times revival.

GLOBAL IMPACT

The Welsh Revival of 1904–5 is such a graphic example of this, because, as H. Elvet Lewis wrote:

It penetrated everywhere and pervaded everything. It was talked of in every railway train, and many a railway compartment became a place of united prayer. . . . Coal mines had their sanctuaries, where prayer-meetings were regularly held, and these prayer meetings had their tales of conversions. It was a weird and winsome scene, when the solemn question was put, "Who is on the Lord's side?" and the safety lamps went up one by one, and when a new lamp was held up in token of a soul changing sides.[6]

By the spring of 1905 the report of what was happening in Wales reached the ears and heart of a holiness preacher in the United States, Frank Bartleman. F. B. Meyer, fresh from the lightning-charged land of Wales, was the messenger. "My heart was stirred to its depths," Bartleman recounted later. He had read of the revival, but now he was getting a direct report. "I then and there promised God He should have full right of way with me, if He could use me."[7]

In the spring of 1905, Bartleman had read S. B. Shaw's *The Great Revival in Wales*.[8] It recorded many direct personal experiences of the Welsh Revival. Reporters were covering it as hard news while other observers were chronicling the impact the revival was having upon them. Among those who commented was the political leader David Lloyd George, who termed the revival "this remarkable upheaval which seems to be rocking Welsh life like a great earthquake."[9] A Methodist journal declared: "Wales is in the throes and ecstasies of the most remarkable religious revival it has ever known."[10]

Through his reading, Bartleman had been struck by a bolt of revival lightning and felt himself aflame. He was so passionate to see revival that he sold copies of Shaw's book in churches all over Los Angeles and Pasadena.[11] The response was positive, and there arose a hunger for revival throughout the area. He also distributed as many as five thousand copies of G. Campbell Morgan's pamphlet, *The Revival in Wales.*

Bartleman met Joseph Smale, the minister of the First Baptist Church of Los Angeles, who had actually visited Wales and wanted to encourage a similar movement in Los Angeles. A result of their meetings was reported by Bartleman in June 1905. Revival had broken out in Los Angeles with meetings "unguided by human hands," and people were being converted "all over the house."[12]

Bartleman wrote Evan Roberts, and Evan responded, though he was inundated with mail. Nevertheless, Evan's short replies "showed his eagerness to keep praying for a worldwide revival."[13] In another letter, Evan told Bartleman that he was praying that God would keep Bartleman's "faith strong" and that the Lord would "save California."[14]

Eventually, Bartleman became a foundational member of the Azusa Street Mission and was destined to play a major part in the modern history of revival.

Meanwhile, in Houston, William J. Seymour, a young African American, was impacted by holiness preacher Charles Parham, who had been moved by pentecostal experiences. In fact, many trace the origins of the pentecostal movement to Parham, but no consideration of modern revival would be complete without reflecting on the importance of William Seymour. Church historian Sidney Ahlstrom described Seymour as manifesting a piety that caused his spiritual impact to be greater even than that of W. E. B. Dubois or Martin Luther King Jr.[15]

Seymour studied with Parham in Houston, and when Neeley Terry, a visitor from Los Angeles, heard Seymour preach, he recommended that Seymour become pastor of his church in California. Seymour preached his first sermon in Los Angeles from Acts 2:4

and told the congregation about the pentecostal manifestations occurring in Houston. When he returned that evening to preach, Seymour found the church doors locked because members were concerned he would bring such phenomena to their church.

Eventually he began ministering to a prayer group meeting in the home of Richard and Ruth Asberry. The group, mostly African Americans with a few white people, earnestly sought God for revival. The ground was building up a charge, and the revival lightning soon struck. On April 9, 1906, there was a powerful manifestation of the Holy Spirit, and the meetings became continual.

Soon the Asberry house could not handle the crowds, and the group—which included Frank Bartleman—moved to a former church building at 312 Azusa Street that had been partially remodeled to include apartments. The convergence of Smale and Bartleman and their knowledge of the Welsh Revival and its inspiration with the ministry of Seymour helped to charge the ground with intensity, and then the bolt struck. It lit a fire that still burns through the pentecostal movement that has covered the world.[16]

The Global South

A 2015 report in the *Washington Post* noted that "one out of 12 people alive today has a pentecostal form of Christian faith." This has resulted in a major demographic change in world Christianity, and the *Post* concluded: "The center of Christianity has shifted from Europe to the global South."[17]

More than one billion people in Africa and Latin America are part of pentecostal communities. The movement in South America especially is rooted in the Azusa Street Revival, which, as we have seen, was inspired and encouraged by the Welsh Revival of 1904–5.

In the groundbreaking book *The Next Christendom*, sociologist Philip Jenkins reported:

> Over the last five centuries, the story of Christianity has been inextricably bound up with Europe and European-derived civilizations overseas, above all in North America. Over the last century, however, the center of gravity in the Christian world has shifted inexorably away from Europe, southward, to Africa and Latin America, and eastward, toward Asia.[18]

"The sheer speed of growth of Pentecostal and charismatic Christianity is difficult to exaggerate," observed Catholic scholar Mathias D. Thelen.[19] He quoted Ralph Martin's opinion:

> By 1992 the numbers of Pentecostals and charismatics had grown to over 410 million and now comprised 24.2 percent of world Christianity. . . . My research has led me to make a bold statement: In all of human history, no other non-political, non-militaristic, voluntary human movement has grown as rapidly as the Pentecostal-charismatic movement in the last 25 years.[20]

There is a form of cosmic radiation, says astrophysics, left over from the moment of creation—called the Big Bang by some. Though creation came long ago, there is a lingering effect of the mighty event. The same is true with revival. Though, as we will discuss in the next chapter, the Welsh Revival of 1904–5 faded, as did all others, they still affect spiritual life across the world today. The radiating energy of the cumulative anointing of revivals through the ages is still at work, still bringing transformation. The pentecostal movement, born in revival, and now expanding at surprising speed, is an example. The rapid growth of Christianity in the global South is the fruit of the waves of revival that have swept the earth many times.

FROM JERUSALEM TO THE REMOTEST PARTS[21]

Jesus commanded His apostles to take the gospel of the kingdom to the farthest reaches of the world. In a way, tiny Wales became a Jerusalem in its time, and almost immediately the spread of the revival was underway.

French pastor Aime Cadot read about what was happening in Wales and went to see. "Bible teachers came from Russia, pastors from Germany and Scandinavia, evangelists from North America and missionaries from India, China, and Africa," wrote Brynmor Pierce Jones.[22] When Evan Roberts traveled to the small village of Hirwaun to hold a meeting, the little place was packed with humanity from around the world. "The little railway station saw a strange sight as the courtyard filled with a mixture of South Africans and Russians, Indians and Irishmen, Norwegians and Dutchmen, and Canadians," Jones noted.[23]

I. V. Neprash, a Russian Christian leader who was later exiled to Siberia, did not directly observe the revival, but he was impacted years later when he came to know Evan Roberts. Neprash had been a pastor in Russia, founded a mission agency focused on reaching Russia, and had served a church in Petrograd. Though he never attended any service of the 1904–5 revival, Neprash was impacted by its radiant afterglow.

"The Welsh Revival was truly a miracle of God," Neprash wrote. One of the confirmations that it was a "God-sent revival" was in the fact that the Holy Spirit was clearly in charge of meetings whether Evan Roberts was present or not.[24] Neprash told of two men who went directly from Wales and the revival to India, where within months thirty thousand people gave their lives to Jesus Christ.

But the revival was moving at a steady pace from its Jerusalem to its Judea and Samaria as well. There were people who had participated in the Welsh Revival who went to Guernsey, an island in the English Channel and a part of Great Britain. Neprash encountered some of their fruit when he later visited Guernsey. He was struck by the fact there were no saloons on the island at that time. Neprash asked a pastor if there was a law against pubs or bars. "None," answered the minister. "The brewers on the Continent tried their best to establish themselves here, spent large sums of money, but failed because of the revival that took possession of the island ten years ago."[25]

Newspapers across other parts of the British Isles and the Continent unwittingly helped in the spread of the revival. "One direct result of this was the increasingly cosmopolitan nature of the revival congregations," wrote Eifion Evans.[26] On a wintery day in February 1905, the isolated village of Nant-y-moel itself experienced a cosmopolitan moment. Three German women arrived who spoke no English and certainly no Welsh. A half dozen Frenchmen had come to the village for the revival meeting, as did a French woman who had been sent by her Paris church to find out what was happening. There were missionaries from China present too. Well-known leaders were also there: F. B. Meyer, G. Campbell Morgan, Gipsy Smith, and other notables.[27]

David Lloyd George noted the revival influence reached Europe, including Paris and down the Italian boot to Naples. The reports were so notorious that the French Home Office decided to check on the sanity of people caught up in the mass excitement. The French public health department dispatched an expert psychiatrist to survey the situation. His report was surprisingly sympathetic. A

French Reformed Church theologian also went to Wales to observe the revival and its effects and wrote: "I profoundly believe that God is really, considerably and undeniably at work in the Welsh Revival. The Spirit of God is here."[28]

Scandinavia felt the radiance of the lightning that had struck Wales. Norwegians were not caught up in the same type of expression as the Welsh, but those who knew the impact of the revival in Norway concluded that "nothing outside of Wales compares with the work which is still in progress in Norway."[29] The lightning struck Sweden early in 1905, and Denmark received the bolt later that year in the autumn.

THE LIGHTNING'S GREAT LEAP

From the icy reaches of Scandinavia to the deserts and jungles of Africa is a long leap, but the power of the revival spanned those great distances. French evangelist Reuben Saillens described the Welsh Revival to large audiences in Algiers, and the impact was such that "by 1906 he could report 'the most encouraging time he had ever known'" in the capital city of Algeria. There were also "indescribable happenings" at the other end of Africa, near Cape Town, as Methodists at a Christian Endeavor meeting in summer 1905 were struck by revival lightning.

The revival leaped southeastward across the globe as people in New Zealand heard about the Welsh Revival in 1905. Though Wales was a world away, there could have been a common bond in places like New Zealand's Waihi mining district as miners heard what has happening to their counterparts in the Welsh coal-mining towns. "Many of the salient features of the Welsh Revival" were present.[30]

In 1904, missionaries in China as well as indigenous Chinese Christians launched a prayer effort to call down the lightning. They prayed that "China might experience a similarly gracious visitation of the Holy Spirit as has recently been seen in Wales." In 1906, workers for Hudson Taylor's China Inland Mission reported that spiritual awakening was occurring. One report noted:

> It is significant that here [in the north of China] and in Shanghai and Canton, the initiative has been so often and so largely Chinese. These revivals have been marked by a wholly unusual conviction of sin and by great anxiety for the conversion of friends and neighbors.[31]

From the Abode of the Clouds to Tropical Jungles

"Nowhere were the revival manifestations repeated with such similarity and intensity as on the Indian mission field of the Calvinist Methodists," noted Eifion Evans.[32] The work he was referring to was mainly in northeast India. There, "Assam had been the particular province of Welsh Presbyterian missionary labour for over sixty years." When they heard reports of the Welsh Revival, "the desire for a time of reviving deepened, and in certain parts of the field many set themselves to pray each night for it."

The gospel of the kingdom had penetrated Cherrapunjee, India, in the mid-nineteenth century through the work of Welsh Calvinist missionaries Thomas and Anna Jones, who landed there on June 22, 1847. The city is in far northeast India, in the hilly state of Meghalaya, which in Sanskrit means "abode of the clouds."

In February 1905, revival lightning struck. "Prayer meetings mushroomed throughout the field as a result of the Assembly, its delegates having returned to pour fresh fuel on an already smoldering fire." People began praying for "an outpouring similar to that experienced in Wales." A correspondent reported: "The Revival has commenced in earnest here, confessing, singing, and praying and all in tears, and determined to live henceforth more worthy of our Lord Jesus Christ. It is now past midnight, and several are now in the chapel singing and praying."[33]

Revival lightning struck in far southern India, a subcontinent away from Assam and Meghalaya. It found ready ground in the churches in Kerala, India's southernmost state. One of those church bodies traced its origins all the way back to AD 52, when it is believed that the apostle Thomas entered what is now the bustling city of Cochin. The apostle planted the church that ultimately adopted his name: the Mar Thoma Church. This great church, now worldwide in scope, includes more than a million and a half members.

Future Indian prime minister Jawaharlal Nehru wrote:

You may be surprised to learn that Christianity came to India long before it went to England or Western Europe, and when even in Rome it was a despised and proscribed sect. Within 100 years or so of the death of Jesus, Christian missionaries came to South India by sea. They were received courteously and permitted to preach their new faith. They converted a large number of people, and their descendants have lived there, with varying fortune, to this day. Most of them belong to old Christian sects which have ceased to exist in Europe.[34]

In the early 1970s I accompanied evangelist John Edmund Haggai, founder of the Haggai Institute, to a Mar Thoma gathering in south India. We found there a distinctive church that describes itself as "Apostolic in origin, Universal in nature, Biblical in faith, Evangelical in principle, Ecumenical in outlook, Oriental in worship, Democratic in nature, and Episcopal in character."

We attended the Maramon Convention, for which Haggai was a speaker. The Mar Thoma Evangelistic Association conducts this meeting every February, with thousands attending. It began in that era when the ground below was calling down the Welsh Revival and other nations were also feeling the approach of revival. Abraham Malpan, the "Martin Luther of the East," was to Kerala what Evan Roberts was to Wales. God used him as a mighty lightning rod in southern India in the nineteenth century, and the Maramon Convention was one of the powerful outcomes.

Decades later I can still hear what to my Western ears was the beautifully exotic and enthusiastic worship and praying of the Maramon multitude gathered under a great arbor constructed amid the lush beauty of a south India tropical landscape.

THE HARD QUESTIONS

Amid reports of all this global vitality, we must pose the following question: While we know the final end-times revival will not fade, *why have all the revivals in the past faded?* In a 2013 paper on the Welsh Revival, Larry Brown cited BBC statistics and found fully one-sixth of the Welsh population claim no religion whatsoever.[35]

> Why do the enterprises we launch with exuberant
>   hope, confident expectation, and visionary aspiration
>   eventually fade?
> How is it that the great fires we light turn into glaciers?

Why do the rockets we launch and the satellites we set in orbit
　　decline and require constant boosts?
Why do our wineskins harden and become brittle?
Why do our thrilling movements ultimately deteriorate into
　　weary institutions?
Is there a spiritual and institutional entropy at work in the
　　fallen world, just as there is the entropy of the second law of
　　thermodynamics in the natural realm?

We tackle these questions in the chapter ahead.

CHAPTER 15

Why Revival Tapers

*The Gospel is not an old, old story, freshly
told. It is a fire in the Spirit, fed by the flame
of Immortal Love; and woe unto us, if, through
our negligence to stir up the Gift of God
which is within us, that fire burns low.*

—LEONARD RAVENHILL

Leonard Ravenhill wrote a classic book titled *Why Revival Tarries.*[1]
But we must explore the question of why revival tapers.

While, as we suggested in the previous chapter, there is a cumulative effect of revival across history, which we compared to cosmic radiation in nature, specific revivals will seem to fade away. After 1905 there was a slow tapering off of the spiritual intensity the principality of Wales had experienced for many months.

If we press the analogy of revival as lightning to its full extent, we come inevitably to the fact that when a bolt strikes, the energy must be captured and conserved, otherwise it dissipates. The same is true of the lightning of revival. Robert Coleman understood spiritual awakening well and wrote, with regard to personal revival, that it "should be a constant reality." But because of "the inconsistent nature of man . . . most of us experience those times of spiritual sluggishness that make revival necessary. But if we live in the continual fullness of the Spirit of Christ, as God desires, revival would be an abiding state."[2]

Sometimes the tapering is caused by human nature itself. The weaknesses of the flesh and the propensity to sin exert a gravitational pull on both personal and corporate revival. Thus Evan Roberts and the Welsh Revival itself came under such gravity and gave occasion for some to mock and discredit both Evan and the revival. Under the stresses of his role, Evan, a man of God but nevertheless a finite human being, became weary.

In late 1905 Evan began suffering from increasing bouts of physical, mental, and emotional exhaustion. During that summer he was struggling within himself about the role he should play in the months ahead. He was "inclining toward the convictions that were presently to remove him from the public stage altogether," wrote R. Tudur Jones.[3] At that point the revival was still ablaze, but "its fervour was not to endure." As Evan passed through his inner turmoil, he became vulnerable to people who would influence him in directions that actually contributed to the tapering of the revival.

GLACIALIZATION

There are two major reasons why revival fades. The first is because the sovereign purposes of God have been achieved and the cloud moves on. The second reason revival tapers and fades is because of human misjudgment and the attempt to trap the fiery revival movement into the cold glacier of institutionalization.

We have used natural lightning as a metaphor for revival, but to best understand the fade of spiritual awakening we draw from another natural phenomenon: glacialization. Great glaciers sometimes form through a dance of fire and ice. Magma arises in the depths of the polar seas in great spears of flame cast up from the earth's core. The frigid water seizes the fire, engulfs its thermodynamic energy, then suffocates the passion of the fire with the cold clutch of the ice.

It is that way geologically, and it is that way institutionally.

THE GREAT FIRE

Almost twenty centuries before the revival lightning set Wales ablaze spiritually, *the* fire erupted in another province of a mighty imperial power: Judea. Jerusalem, Nazareth, Capernaum, Tiberius, the Ten Cities, Jericho, and other sites were hit by the flame. Jesus of Nazareth was the living bolt that appeared from the expansive cloud of eternity and sparked the great fire. For three years He burst into the obscure towns and cities in a strip of land Rome subjugated and would have preferred not to think about at all. But the fire could not be ignored. Its flames licked at the cold structures of civil, social, and religious authoritarianism, blistering the totalitarian elites sheltered in the ice until they had to try to put out the blaze.

The flames bursting out from the great central blaze set others afire, and they emerged from the conflagration to add to the torment of the elites. Something had to be done. In a rare collusion, the establishments of civil governance, society, and religion determined to snuff out the great fire that spread its intensity to all the others. The bonfire smoldered three days, and then burst again into flame—this time even more intensely.

And one day known in the religious and cultural calendar of that land as Pentecost, tongues of flame ignited a movement. Like a prairie fire, it spread with furious intensity until at last it blazed in the very heart of the world, burning out the landscape of old, rotting growth, and leaving in its searing wake the nurturing ashes that would bring about the new. The ice dwellers feared the blaze because it threatened the glacial caves in which they felt safe and sheltered.

In time, people realized the flame could not be put out, and they began to consider how to harness it. Slowly what was once a purifying, energizing fire, like the magma arising in Arctic seas, was encased in the icy grip of the glacier of institutionalism that chills revival.

This very problem sparked Jesus' intense reactions to the Pharisees and general religious establishment of Judaism in the first century. Jesus lit a flame on the glacial surface of religion in that day with such heat that its leaders wanted to kill Him. They complained about Jesus' disciples picking grain on the Sabbath, and He seared their cold hearts with the retort, "The Sabbath was made for man, and not man for the Sabbath" (Mark 2:27). That is, humans are not made for institutions but institutions for human beings. The totalitarians who rule over the bastions of institutionalism saw it otherwise. People are cogs for the state, fodder for the labor force, supplicants for the religious system. Jesus, however, seared the very heart of the glacier.

In the midst of the 1960s tempest, Findley Edge became a leading expert on the process of what we term here *glacialization*. Edge spoke especially of it as the institutionalization of the church. He outlined the process by which a movement with all its fiery passion could harden into a cold institution.

Movements arise in the fire. "Generally a movement is born in a time of great stress as a violent reaction against errors, abuses, and the injustices in the status quo," Edge wrote.[4] The zealots of reform run into opposition and persecution from the institutions of the status quo. But those committed to the movement are so passionate they are willing to suffer and even to die.

Movement leaders are determined that their crusade must not fade. They begin to develop plans, strategies, and even their own institutional forms to perpetuate their cause. The zealots have two goals: (1) the meaning and message of the movement must be propagated to others and (2) its principles must be passed on to future generations. The movement experiences *rapid growth.* The status quo is threatened as expansion occurs mainly among people who feel disenfranchised or see themselves as outsiders with respect to the status quo establishments. The movement, according to Edge, becomes a "hated sect" and passes into a season of *persecution* by the institutions determined to protect the interests of the status quo.

Next comes a dangerous stage as the movement begins to be *tolerated* by the status quo. The establishment does not like it, but because many are joining, it is forced into reluctant toleration. The danger for the movement now is that it discovers how nice it is not to be thrown to the lions or imprisoned. Next, there is broad *acceptance* of the movement. Compromise enters as people within the movement begin to consider how to sustain and enlarge the new recognition by society at large. There is cross-fertilization between the once new ideas and the old traditions. This results in dilution so that, Edge said, "There is not now as much difference between the two [the movement and the old status quo] as at the beginning."[5]

The last stage for what was once a distinct movement is *popularity.* The trend toward centralization develops during this stage. Size, complexity, and control become important. Those within what was once a movement and who disagree with the acquiescence to the status quo are now regarded as outsiders. Bureaucracies develop, populated by careerists who fret about insurance, pensions, putting their kids through school, and all the other demands of earning a living. Their survival becomes their primary focus, and since their well-being is tied to the institution, its perpetuation is of utmost importance.

When the survival of the institution becomes more important than the fresh ideas that birthed the original movement, institutionalization has occurred. A new glacier has been calved out of what was once fire and fury.

THE REFORMATION EXAMPLE

Findley Edge traced how it happened to Judaism and how the Jesus movement emerged from the institutionalization of that religion. Then it happened to the Jesus movement as it hardened into the glacial institutionalism that provoked Martin Luther into his fiery passion for reform. Sadly, Luther and his movement ultimately became glacial.

There is much in the history of the Welsh Revival of 1904–5 to suggest that the glacialization of institutionalization contributed to the tapering off of the revival movement. A brief look at what happened to Luther's reform movement, sparked more than three hundred years earlier, deepens our understanding of what happened to Evan Roberts and the Welsh Revival and what lurks continually as a threat to all spiritual awakening movements.

"Revivals are often overlooked as significant contributors to the Reformation," wrote revival scholars Malcolm McDow and Alvin L. Reid.[6] They point to revivals under Peter Waldo and Francis of Assisi in the twelfth century, John Tauler, John Huss and John Wycliffe in the fourteenth century, and Girolamo Savonarola in the fifteenth century as precursors to Luther's Reformation, which was sparked in the sixteenth century.

Revivals, therefore, "were indispensable contributors of the Reformation," McDow and Reid observed. But the Reformation "in turn provided the atmosphere for the subsequent revivals in Christian history."[7] They noted this was also the case in the Old Testament. The reformation of worship under Josiah, for example, drew the lightning of revival in Judah. In another chapter we discussed the revival cycle, and here we see a subcycle within the larger: revival leads to reformation that leads to revival. The Reformation of the sixteenth century not only "altered church practices and changed doctrinal beliefs but also created spiritual cradles in human hearts that became the depositories for spiritual awakening."[8]

But there is a caveat: revival leads to reformation that leads to revival *unless* either of those fires is snuffed out in the icebergs of institutionalism. This, in fact, is why the Reformation occurred. The medieval Roman Catholic Church was an imposing institution, but it seemed to have forgotten Jesus' principle discussed elsewhere in these pages that the institution was made for people, not people for the institution. Thus,

> Instead of standing against oppression, it oppressed; instead of protection, coercion; instead of mercy, condemnation; instead of love, persecution; instead of understanding, intolerance; instead of hope, hopelessness; instead of salvation by grace, constraints that shackled the spirit; instead of pointing people to Christ, it pointed people to itself; instead of extending compassion, it exercised control.[9]

All these were characteristics of the institutionalization that had made the church—that had been electrified and energized at Pentecost and had set the Roman Empire on fire—into a ponderous lump of ice, freezing the landscape. At the outset of the Reformation movement, Luther might not have believed that the icy tentacles would reach into the movement's many fires and snuff them out in their chill grip. It's not likely that one could have convinced Evan Roberts during the intense early lightning strikes across Wales that the day would come when the bolts would be entombed in ice. Had he studied the outcomes for Luther and the Reformation, he might have had greater insight and discernment about the directions of the movement for which he had been given major stewardship.

Luther's world was trembling with the ferocious dance of fire and ice. It was a civilization all at once ablaze with change yet also characterized by the hardening of the icy institutionalism.

Luther's Reformation would meet the surging streams of two other movements of the sixteenth century: the Renaissance and political upheaval. The Renaissance was plowing the riverbed toward humanism while power rivalries were threatening disunity.

In the era leading up to Luther's Reformation, Johannes Gutenberg introduced what we would call an upgrade to the printing process. Speed and efficiency of publishing and spreading information were the results of Gutenberg's advances. While Luther's era might not match the scope and intensity of the current information age, it was every bit as powerful in reshaping communications and disseminating data. Ultimately, the new media would make Luther an international figure.

One of the greatest impacts was the way Gutenberg's new process affected the style of media and composition. Today we recognize the alterations computer talk has made to our message, especially when it comes to social media and the terse 140-character shorthand style to which we are often bound. Prior to Gutenberg's innovations, printing focused on ponderous intellectual works. But when Luther sat down to pen the Ninety-Five Theses, he was actually thinking—maybe unconsciously—of the new printing medium by which his words would ultimately be transmitted. Perhaps this explains the tight style of the Theses. If so, Luther had become an early example of what Marshall McLuhan termed more than four hundred years later "the medium is the message." Had Luther's theses been written in the turgid academic style of the old printing style, they may not have had the large impact on the popular mind.

The knowledge base that would pour into and through Gutenberg's new information system was also increasing rapidly. By 1492 it was clear to many the earth was a sphere, not a flat disc. Martin Behaim designed a globe that provided a graphic depiction of the new understanding of the earth. Christopher Columbus tested the concept and did not fall off the edge of the world. Nicolaus Copernicus then shook that world by contending that the planetary system in our planet's cosmic neighborhood was not centered on the earth but the sun. The glacial institution of the church trembled at such thought. Giordano Bruno would develop Copernicus's theory and ultimately be burned at the stake.

Pocket watches began ticking in Luther's world—if not his breeches—seventeen years before he nailed the Ninety-Five Theses to the Castle Church door. In Italy, Leonardo da Vinci was tinkering with the idea that humans might be able to fly. While they could not soar around the world on wings, schools of explorers cut their way through the seas: Columbus westward to the New World, Vasco de Gama eastward to India, and two years after Luther's hammer struck the church door, Ferdinand Magellan circumnavigated the globe.

All the while, however, ecclesiastical correctness (EC) was

hardening like a massive iceberg riding this tumultuous sea of change roaring with the fires of exploration and discovery. The big ice mountain sought to block the currents and it would not move. Like all glacial formations there were many frozen layers to the EC institutionalization of Luther's day:

* The establishment of human dogma over truth.
* The substitution of authoritarianism for true authority.
* A move from God-centeredness to human-centeredness.
* The reversal of Jesus' priority of people over institutions.
* The elevation of the trivial over the crucial.

What is striking is how these same elements forming the glacier of religious ecclesiastical correctness in Luther's day and again in the time of the Welsh Revival are present in the secular political correctness of our time. Human-contrived relativism has displaced absolute truth, authoritarianism has pushed aside true authority, human-centeredness displayed graphically in the rise of the selfie culture has replaced the focus on God, ironically, at the same time as PC institutions quash people who oppose their mandates, and trivialities have triumphed over that which is truly crucial.

POLITICAL CORRECTNESS AND THE WELSH REVIVAL

By 1905, an underlying political correctness of both theology and style was closing in on the Welsh Revival. There were needed corrections from credible and respected critics who continued to support Evan and the revival. On the other hand, there were attempts to encase Evan and the revival into institutional molds. Some were direct and up-front, lacking any subtlety or hidden motives. Both J. Vynrwy Morgan and Peter Price fell into that category. Other efforts to gain control over Evan and the revival were subtle, indirect, and even covert. Sadly, Jessie Penn-Lewis seemed to be a major force in this category.

Penn-Lewis's influence on Evan and the revival was toward institutionalization. "It seems probable that Jessie Penn-Lewis played a significant part in bringing the great Welsh revival to a premature end, even though she seemed to have had the best of intentions," Rick Joyner observed.[10] Joyner cites J. C. Metcalfe's foreword to *War on the Saints*, the book coauthored by Penn-Lewis and Roberts to show what was driving Penn-Lewis's efforts to corral Evan and the revival:

> An aftermath of the Welsh Revival at the dawn of the present century was the rise of a number of extreme cults, often stressing a return to "Pentecostal" practices. Mrs. Penn-Lewis, who had witnessed much of the revival as the representative of The Life of Faith, saw clearly the peril of these fanatical teachings, and in collaboration with Mr. Evan Roberts, who played so prominent a Part in the revival, wrote a book, *War on the Saints*. In this book, these extreme and overbalanced beliefs and practices are categorically branded as the work of an invading host of evil spirits. The word "deception" might be said to be the key word of the book.

These were doubtless the "best of intentions," Joyner said, but Penn-Lewis's position "is both reactionary and sown with idealism."[11]

The reactionary element was revealed in Penn-Lewis's aim to get Evan out of the revival because of what she perceived as excess, and the idealism was in her apparent belief that the movement could be improved if it were more institutionalized.

Evan met Jessie Penn-Lewis at a vulnerable point in his life and ministry. Criticisms that had been thrust at him had wounded his soul. He was "depressed most of the time," wrote Roberts Liardon,[12] who viewed Penn-Lewis as a "Jezebel" as she introduced herself to Evan at the Keswick meeting. She did not enjoy a good reputation in Wales "due to serious doctrinal conflicts," said Liardon. Some who were exposed to Penn-Lewis's teachings on suffering felt they veered from sound doctrine and did not want her teaching in Wales.

Liardon and others believed Penn-Lewis wanted to align herself with Evan "to gain his acceptance." Like herself, Evan had been "shattered," she told some of her friends, and needed a "getaway." Evan retreated to the Penn-Lewis country home and not long afterward suffered his fourth breakdown. Evan was so immobilized it took a year before he could stand up, let alone walk.[13]

Evan was completely sequestered in the Penn-Lewis home in England. They erected a new house at Leicester and included for Evan a bedroom, prayer room, and his own stairs. Visitors were restricted, including, at times, members of Evan's own family. Penn-Lewis apparently kept Evan from knowing that his mother was critically sick in Wales. Evan's father traveled to England to visit his son, but Evan himself would not meet with him because Evan's great spiritual task meant even eschewing his blood kin.

Evan stayed inside the Penn-Lewis home for eight years. It was as if Penn-Lewis encased him—the man who had once been a lightning rod drawing God's fire upon his country—inside a glacier. Penn-Lewis convinced Evan that the spiritual dynamics associated with his revival ministry were not of God and that he had been deceived.

Penn-Lewis wrote to another revival leader that Evan needed to be "safeguarded." Under the new arrangements he was growing spiritually at a "great rate." She was convinced that she and Evan were undergoing training "for a special work."[14]

PRIMARY MARK OF INSTITUTIONALIZATION

The tragic relationship between Evan Roberts and Jessie Penn-Lewis reveals the primary mark of institutionalization. Apparently Penn-Lewis was trying to preserve her own ministry (as we saw, a prime indicator of institutionalization emerges when the survival of the institution becomes more important than the movement from which it was birthed). Penn-Lewis seemed to have tried to hook the heavy load of her own ministerial survival on the movement of which Evan was a major leader, and both were pulled down. Soon Penn-Lewis and Evan launched *The Overcomer*, a journal mailed to five thousand people around the world. Among its themes was the assertion that some practices of pentecostals were "satanic."[15]

During the period of Evan's "encasement," Penn-Lewis would sometimes sit at his bedside and encourage him to recount his visions and dreams along with voices he had heard. She linked these with bizarre behaviors and mistakes Evan had made, and he became increasingly convinced that he had been deceived. But Penn-Lewis told him (revealing the core message that would be developed in *War on the Saints*):

> The more spiritual he is, the more open he is to spirits, evil or good. If any believer will seek an experience of the Cross, Satan will give him the desired thing. Then the evidence of the false leading shows up, namely doubts and agitations, and a kind of self-exaltation because they have this feeling that God is going

to do great things through them because they have been summoned. This is deception.[16]

The outcome was that Evan "would distrust mystical experiences, and would claim that things such as tongues and prophesyings and visions were not safe until believers had far greater wisdom and experience."[17] Increasingly, Evan's thinking was becoming more institutional.

Was Penn-Lewis wrong in her warnings? Certainly, in light of strange actions and the importance of resisting the pull toward "frenzy," as we discussed in a previous chapter, restraints and boundaries are important. Evan *did* need guidance. But the *method* by which Evan was receiving this counsel was wrong, and it resulted in his taking a hard turn toward "form," which, in the extreme, is the utter encasement in a glacial institutionalism.

The better way to receive instruction—and maintain the vitality of a movement—is given in Paul's letter to Titus, leader of the church in Crete, a wild and boisterous society at that time (see Titus 1:10–16). Paul's instruction was to set the church "in order," by appointing "elders in every city as I directed you" (Titus 1:5). Then Paul listed the qualifications for the elders:

[Elders should be] above reproach, the husband of one wife, having children who believe, not accused of dissipation or rebellion. . . . Not self-willed, not quick-tempered, not addicted to wine, not pugnacious, not fond of sordid gain, but hospitable, loving what is good, sensible, just, devout, self-controlled, holding fast the faithful word which is in accordance with the teaching, so that he will be able both to exhort in sound doctrine and to refute those who contradict. (Titus 1:6–9)

An outside revivalist working in a church where he or she is a guest should, in New Testament order, minister under the authority of the elders in that local congregation, beginning with the lead elder, the senior pastor. Later critiques and teaching should also come to a minister of the Word—whether a traveling evangelist or teacher—through an established eldership. Sometimes there might be a council, reaching across the body of Christ, to guide key leaders touching a wide part of the church, as in New Testament times and the early history of the church.

The greatest time of improvement for Evan during the period of his "encasement" in the Penn-Lewis home was when R. B. Jones came to see him. Jones was reluctant at first, but finally journeyed to Leicester. He was, per Brynmor Pierce Jones's description, "universally respected as a revival teacher"—a true elder.[18]

Later, the Penn-Lewises took Evan on holiday to Davos, Switzerland. From there, she wrote R. B. Jones a letter. "From the day that you visited Leicester, he has steadily gained and now he is able to think freely," she said. Evan himself appreciated Jones's ministry to him, and wrote encouraging notes pledging his personal prayers as Jones was in America, visiting chapels in Pennsylvania.[19]

It is vital that the church today learn how to maintain biblical order that does not harden into suffocating institutionalization. There is a great revival coming that will stretch the wineskins everywhere. We could even call it a jubilee!

CHAPTER 16

Jubilee!

Something great is on the horizon.
—ROBERT COLEMAN[1]

God is up to something big.
—TOM PHILLIPS[2]

I began this book by describing the moment the lightning of personal revival fell on me in 1974 while serving a church in Spanish Fort, Alabama, on Mobile Bay. We return there now, at the conclusion of this book, to a sublime, aptly named town a few miles south of Spanish Fort: Fairhope. The pier at Fairhope is one of my favorite places to go to breathe, rest, and think. A half century later, after a long drive from our home in Houston, Fairhope Pier is one of the places I want to visit first.

My memories go back to spectacular July 4 fireworks extravagances played out over the pier, dancing on the waters with stunning hues, and also balmy evenings when the stresses of pastoring a church vaporized in the mists rising from the bay as Irene and I strolled hand-in-hand out to the pier's edge.

And I always think of the men and women who get up early, hike out to the end of the pier, and stay until the last shard of sunlight dives over the western reaches of Mobile Bay. Just about any time of the day, fishers will be out there. Their bait buckets are full, sometimes a fish jerks at the end of their line, and the conversation falls pleasantly on the ear with South Alabama lingo, a tasty blend of African American, Cajun, Creole, and good ol' boy.

In that beautiful world for just a moment, there is no racism, nobody thinks of political conflict, religious strife, or anything that divides the fisher folk. If you get a fishhook stuck in your finger, everybody will suddenly become doting nurses, skilled surgeons, and fellow sufferers who assure you they survived their fishhook punctures and surely you will too.

Eventually the conversation on the pier almost always comes to the great hope of the fishing folk—*Jubilee!*

THE JUBILEE VISION

One day, many years ago, I stood on the edge of the bay near Fairhope pier and had a mighty jubilee vision of the coming revival. That vision—like the Holy Spirit's lightning bolt I told you about at the beginning of this book—has not left me and still thrills my heart more than four decades later.

As a pastor in the region for four years I had heard the tales of jubilee, perhaps the ultimate fish story. Periodically, all the aquatic life in Mobile Bay surges to the shore. Someone will catch the flurry on the waters and shout, "Jubilee!" The message, even in the days before social media, flashes up and down the bay, from Fairhope to Spanish Fort, down to Bayou la Batre and throughout Baldwin County. People quickly grab washtubs, baskets, buckets, anything to handle the harvest.

Mobile Bay is home to 125 species of aquatic life. Everything out there comes in: the good stuff like whitefish, mullet, shrimp, redfish, sheepshead, flounder, crab, and what some might think of as the not-so-good and scary-looking Gulf sturgeon, madly flopping small shark, stingrays, and slithering eels. Everybody who comes to the jubilee ready to haul in the aquatic harvest gets all they can handle and more. I have stood at the spot near the Fairhope Pier many times and scanned the waters, hoping I would see the splashes and rush of foam and have the privilege of being the first to shout "Jubilee!"

I never did. But on that special day, I saw something greater. The Holy Spirit seemed to be saying that jubilee is the nature of the great coming revival. It will be sudden. It will be a great blessing. Everything "out there" will come in, and all who are prepared with their nets and buckets and tubs will reap the harvest of those rushing toward the shore of salvation.

Death awaits the fish bounding to the bay's shoreline, but in the jubilee of the coming revival, there will be life abundant and eternal awaiting on the shore for all who come in.

This is exactly what happened in the Welsh Revival. Well-dressed businessmen could be seen kneeling at altars, their shoulders rubbing against the grimy overalls of miners just off their shifts. Young people regarded as hooligans joined in worship with choir-boys and girls. Women of questionable character lifted up prayer right next to women who gossiped about them. Scholars with a caravan of degrees chasing their names might be enthralled by the preaching of Evan Roberts, who had barely six weeks of preparatory school readying him for the "higher" education he never received.

In our day, churches will have to stretch their own arms of compassion and sheltering mercy wings. Drug addicts, gender-confused, tattooed, skinheads, refugees from the hook-up culture, GQ-fashioned young men, girls whose clothes leave little to the imagination, thieves, abused women and children, abusers of women and children, drunkards, formerly proud church folk shocked to discover their religious fervor would not save them, politicians, publicans.

In other words, everything out there in the contemporary culture at that moment.

CRISIS AND JUBILEE

What compels the rush to shore by the aquatic life of Mobile Bay is a change in the waters that constitutes a crisis. In 1973, biologist Edwin May sought the specific causes of the Mobile Bay jubilee. He found that weather phenomena affected the tides and current, causing a drop in the oxygen supply. Fish get trapped between the shore and the water beyond that is low in oxygen. The aquatic life comes to the surface in search of oxygen, and they surge toward the shore where it is in greater abundance.[3]

As we have seen in the lightning analogy throughout this book, there is a buildup in the ground below that draws the lightning. That buildup intensifies crisis. The immediate result is anxiety, then fear, then desperation. This is what finally prompts people to intercede seriously for God's intervention.

In 1974, Billy Graham addressed the Lausanne Congress on Global Evangelization. He talked about this relationship between crisis and revival:

I believe there are two strains in prophetic Scripture. One leads us to understand that as we approach the latter days and the Second Coming of Christ, things will become worse and worse. Joel speaks of "multitudes, multitudes in the valley of decision!" The day of the Lord is near in the valley of decision. He is speaking of judgment.

But I believe as we approach the latter days and the coming of the Lord, it could be a time also of great revival. We cannot forget the possibility and the promise of revival, the refreshing of the latter days of the outpouring of the Spirit promised in Joel 2:28 and repeated in Acts 2:17. That will happen right up to the advent of the Lord Jesus Christ.

Evil will grow worse, but God will be mightily at work at the same time.[4]

Thus we see again the linear-cyclical nature of time in the interaction between *kronos* and *kairos*, which we discussed in a previous chapter. Crisis and revival appear in sequence all across history. They intensify as they move toward the *telos* (purpose and goal) of all history. This interaction of crisis and revival, as Graham said, "will happen right up to the end of history." Again, this is the very point Jesus made in Matthew 24:14, when He said the gospel of the kingdom would be proclaimed in all the world as a witness to all the nations and then the end (*telos*) will come.

We should live with a continual expectancy of revival, all the way to the consummate revival—the coming of the Lord Jesus Christ!

The Lord Himself inserted the Jubilee idea in His address at Nazareth at the inauguration of His earthly ministry. That day at the synagogue, Jesus read from Isaiah, presenting Himself to the shock and dismay of the congregation as its fulfilment:

The Spirit of the Lord is upon Me,
Because He anointed Me to preach the gospel to
    the poor.
He has sent Me to proclaim release to the captives,
And recovery of sight to the blind,
To set free those who are oppressed,
To proclaim the favorable year of the Lord. (Luke 4:18–19)

The Old Testament Background

To the Hebrew ears listening to Jesus that day in Nazareth, mention of "the favorable year of the Lord" would have brought to mind the ancient command of God to observe a Jubilee every fifty years:

> You are also to count off seven sabbaths of years for yourself, . . . namely, forty-nine years. You shall then sound a ram's horn abroad on the tenth day of the seventh month; on the day of atonement you shall sound a horn all through your land. You shall thus consecrate the fiftieth year and proclaim a release through the land to all its inhabitants. It shall be a jubilee for you. (Lev. 25:8–10)

The Hebrew word for "jubilee" actually points to the blasts of trumpets and horns that announce a celebration or special event. In the Old Testament, then, the Jubilee commands of God summon the people to a special era marked by celebration because of the delightful new behaviors and actions that will characterize it.

Thus, in His inaugural message at the synagogue in Nazareth, Jesus is announcing the coming of the new Jubilee season, one that will never end. This was and is the greatest news ever, but the people at the synagogue that day were so blinded and deafened with their misconceptions, presuppositions about Jesus, son of Mary and Joseph, all transmitted through the town rumor mill, that they missed the trumpet call. Instead, they wanted to silence the joyful announcement of "the favorable year of the LORD."

Everything in the Old Testament points to Jesus Christ and the New Covenant. The Old Testament is a trail of crumbs leading us to the Bread of Life. It's no wonder Jesus announces His ministry at Nazareth by bringing to mind the Jubilee that now becomes a new season in time, ushered in by His coming into the world and His work here, culminating in the Atonement.

The Jubilee proclaimed by Jesus is the conjunction of *kairos* and *kronos*, the intersection in human time of the opportune moment when heaven engages with earth. Every true revival is a manifestation of this and thus is an interaction with God and humanity in the arena of human history.

The Jubilee foreshadows those periods when the cloud of God's glory hovers over the earth and releases its revival lightning in the ground below that calls it down. The themes of the Old Testament Jubilee describe what happens in true revival, which the 1904–5 Welsh experience shows so abundantly.

Rededication

God's command to the Hebrews was that they "consecrate the fiftieth year" as the Jubilee (Lev. 25:10). The Hebrew word means to "hallow" something, treating it with respect and reverence. The idea of separation is embedded in the term, as in setting something apart as holy.

God's call in revival Jubilee is for men and women to focus on God's transcendent majesty, to once again reverence Him. The pull of the fallen world trapped in finitude is always on the immanent scale—and then downward. Revival, as we have seen, lifts the human perspective. People begin to see themselves and their actions from the perspective of God's purity and develop a hunger for righteousness.

After their exhaustive study of the history of revivals, Malcolm McDow and Alvin L. Reid wrote:

> If we are to see an awakening in our day, let the revival for which we pray be a revival of holiness—a revival marked by an awesome respect for a sovereign God, brokenness over individual sin, and a passion for obedience. . . . While different details can be gleaned from various movements, one thing is constant: the holiness of a sovereign God.[5]

Release

In addition to dedicating the fiftieth year as a Jubilee before the Lord, Israel was commanded to "proclaim a release through the land to all its inhabitants" (Lev. 25:10). Debts were to be forgiven and people were to relate to one another, not with exploitation in mind, but in the context of the liberty proclaimed by God Himself.

This points to the great liberty that comes in Jesus Christ through His grace. It is also freedom from oppression and control, whether by human against human or the captivation by demons. During the Welsh Revival, as we have seen, the power of addictions was broken. Drunkards were set free. Gamblers were no longer under bondage and could now support their families.

Return

The Lord declared to the Hebrews that in the Jubilee year, "Each of you shall return to his own property, and each of you shall return to his family" (Lev. 25:10).

During the Welsh Revival, William Hughes, a rough miner

forced out of work by management, returned to God and that returned him to himself and his family. Before he was struck by the revival bolt, Hughes occasionally went home, but most often he wandered in Scotland and England, far from his family. The man had lived a "reckless life," recalled H. Elvet Lewis. One night, however, in his tormented travels, Hughes stumbled into a revival meeting where Dan Roberts, Evan's brother, was preaching. Hughes had come under deep conviction, and though he didn't know it, two revival workers had been watching him struggle and were praying for him. Hughes left the service and headed for a tavern, hoping a drink could squelch the roiling in his soul. But something displaced the yearning for drink, and he pushed it away.

Later, deep in another mine where he had managed to find work, Hughes was actually shivering because of the tumult inside him. "What's the matter?" a coworker asked. "I don't know," Hughes replied. "I'll tell you what it is," his companion said. "The Holy Spirit has got hold of you."

The workmate left, and Hughes's conviction intensified. Finally he cried to God for mercy and strength. "And as he cried he felt as if a physical burden were being lifted from him. . . . Tears came, but their bitterness was gone," Lewis recorded Hughes's testimony. The first thing Hughes did was hurry home, where his children were amazed and his wife was afraid the change in him was too good to be true. But it was true, so much so that "he became the evangelist of his kindred." The home that was headed for dissolution became "a surgery of wounded souls."[6]

Redemption

In the Jubilee declaration to the Israelites, the Lord said: "The land, moreover, shall not be sold permanently, for the land is Mine; for you are but aliens and sojourners with Me. Thus for every piece of your property, you are to provide for the redemption of the land" (Lev. 25:23–24).

Demons are constantly searching for place, as we discussed in an earlier chapter. They want the property of our very being. The desire of the placeless fallen angels who have left their own abode is to inhabit and control the territory of our lives. Because humanity chooses sin, and because we individually sell ourselves into sin every time we make a choice from the freedom of our own will to sin, the demons believe they own us.

But Jesus Christ came to redeem us from that satanic owner-ship. The life is in the blood (Lev. 17:11), and our own blood was the river on which the demonic could sail through our souls and bodies. In true revival, people meet Jesus. They may not know the-ology, but the Holy Spirit draws them to Jesus Christ and freedom. His blood becomes the redemptive price and replaces the spiritually diseased bloodstream that has given the demonic a title deed to our very being.

As mentioned in an earlier chapter, newspaper editor W. T. Stead reported on the earliest days of the Welsh Revival. As he traveled through south Wales, he was struck by testimonies like that of Florrie Evans. "This public self-consecration, this definite and decisive avowal of a determination to put under their feet their dead past of vice and sin and indifference, and to reach out towards a higher ideal of human existence, is going on everywhere in Wales," he related.

Repentance is a turning away from sin and a turning to Christ and His righteousness. Stead found evidences of that true repentance in the miners in the small village of Mardy. He spent a Sunday there in December 1904 and reported that "the miners are voluntarily tax-ing themselves this year three half-pence in the pound of their weekly wages to build an institute, public hall, library, and reading room."[7]

True revival leads to true repentance.

Regard

In His Jubilee commands, God told the Hebrews: "You shall thus observe My statutes and keep My judgments, so as to carry them out, that you may live securely in the land" (Lev. 25:18). Here God calls for the linkage of orthodoxy (right belief) with orthopraxy (right action, work). This is the kind of authentic faith that James writes about under the Spirit's inspiration:

> What use is it, my brethren, if someone says he has faith but he has no works? Can that faith save him? If a brother or sister is without clothing and in need of daily food, and one of you says to them, "Go in peace, be warmed and filled," and yet you do not give them what is necessary for their body, what use is that? Even so faith, if it has no works, is dead, being by itself. (James 2:14–17)

God's statutes and judgments are the practical guides for carrying out the new spirit brought through true revival. If there is no impact on society, a movement cannot be considered authentic revival, since the fruit will be manifested in the everyday lives of people impacted by revival.

All the meetings throughout Wales, with singing, praying, shouting, dancing, and falling to the floor, would be merely emotional phenomena if there were no new regard for God's ways to be put into practice for the sake of the nation. However, as Elvet Lewis wrote, there were widespread impacts on the quality of life during and in the aftermath of the Welsh Revival until the movement was encased in the institutionalism we spoke of earlier:

> While in England and other countries the Church laments the estrangement of the working classes, in Wales, at the dawn of

the twentieth century, these, in their thousands, helped to create a movement whose end is not yet. Miners and quarrymen, field laborers and tin-workers, the whole artisanry of the Welsh nation, which means, of course, the over-whelming majority of it, joined in one immense prayer-meeting from north to south, from east to west.[8]

A Coming Jubilee?

Is there, then, an even greater Jubilee revival in the world's future?

Tom Phillips, vice president of the Billy Graham Evangelistic Association, noted scattered bolts of revival in our age. It made him think of his growing-up years on a Mississippi farm. "Today, when I look at the national landscape called the American church, I sense the childhood anticipation of the harvest building once again," Phillips wrote. "Although I feel the anticipation, already I know the answers. It was the same one I heard as a farm child looking for an earlier harvest. Wait."[9]

How long?

Both Billy Graham and revival and evangelism scholar Robert Coleman stress the linkage between Joel 2:28–29 and Acts 2:16–18.

> I will pour out My Spirit on all mankind;
> And your sons and daughters will prophesy,
> Your old men will dream dreams,
> Your young men will see visions.
> Even on the male and female servants
> I will pour out My Spirit in those days. (Joel 2:28–29)

Peter quotes this passage in his Pentecost message:

"AND IT SHALL BE IN THE LAST DAYS," GOD SAYS,
"THAT I WILL POUR FORTH OF MY SPIRIT ON ALL MANKIND;
AND YOUR SONS AND YOUR DAUGHTERS SHALL PROPHESY,
AND YOUR YOUNG MEN SHALL SEE VISIONS,
AND YOUR OLD MEN SHALL DREAM DREAMS;
EVEN ON MY BONDSLAVES, BOTH MEN AND WOMEN,
I WILL IN THOSE DAYS POUR FORTH OF MY SPIRIT." (Acts
2:17–18)

Coleman sees these passages as "a statement clearly indicating that all classes of people from the world will feel the impact of spiritual rejuvenation," but he pointed out, "the universal dimension of the prophecy of Joel was not experienced fully in that the Spirit did not come upon God's people all over the world."[10]

And there are other prophecies and passages to be considered, according to Coleman:

+ A global revival would certainly be consistent with God's "all-embracing love" as Jesus described it in John 3:16.
+ It would seem an essential part of the Lord's command to go into all the world, to the uttermost (Matt. 28:18–20; Acts 1:8).
+ Global revival would seem to fulfill the promise God made to Abraham that all the world's peoples would be blessed in him and his seed—pointing ultimately to Jesus Christ (Gen. 12:3; 22:18).
+ All the families of the earth worshipping God would actually happen under a global revival (Ps. 22:27; 86:9; Isa. 49:6; Dan. 7:14; Rev. 15:4).
+ Worldwide spiritual awakening would bring to pass Malachi's prophecy that God's name would be great among the Gentiles from the rising to the setting of the sun (Mal. 1:11).

✦ Habakkuk's prophecy that "the earth will be filled with the knowledge of the glory of the LORD, as the waters cover the sea" (Hab. 2:14) would be fulfilled.[11]

Such a harmonious witness across the Scriptures sparks expectation among many, such as Jonathan Edwards, Isaac Watts, William Carey, Henry Martyn, and Charles Simeon.[12]

"Scripture does point to some kind of climactic spiritual conflagration, though the time and extent of its coming can be variously understood," Coleman noted. "The day is envisioned when the Church in all parts of the world will know the overflow of God's presence."[13]

Long ago the prophet Zechariah wrote:

> Thus says the LORD of hosts, "It will yet be that peoples will come, even the inhabitants of many cities. The inhabitants of one will go to another, saying, 'Let us go at once to entreat the favor of the LORD, and to seek the LORD of hosts; I will also go.' So many peoples and mighty nations will come to seek the LORD of hosts in Jerusalem and to entreat the favor of the LORD." (Zech. 8:20–22)

What would happen if the global Christian community gathered at Jerusalem, whether the actual city in Israel or the spiritual, in local rallies in cities everywhere, or at a vast coming together in cyberspace via the internet to seek the favor of God for worldwide revival?

I believe revival would come! Bigger than we have ever seen: nations, governments, churches, businesses, families, marriages, schools. Institutions of every kind. All would be changed. God will have initiated a global outpouring of His Spirit. The greatest revival in history would be upon us.

One suspects that after such a united voice calling down lightning that the next action would be to scan the horizon and watch for the cloud and the lightning . . . and get ready for Jubilee!

> And there will be very many fish; . . . everything will live where the river goes. And it will come about that fishermen will stand beside it; from Engedi to Eneglaim there will be a place for the spreading of nets. Their fish will be according to their kinds, like the fish of the Great Sea, very many. (Ezek. 47:9–10)

While, like you, I can see all the signs, I'm not fearful. What I see is a forerunner to what God has called us to do. The end times is not just a series of events that we have no control over. Instead, it should be a motivating factor in getting involved with what God is preparing for these years. If we want to be a part of it, then let's get busy.

Afterglow

It's a long way from Wales to a maximum-security prison in Brazil or a slum on the backstreets of one of its cities. But Michael and Hazel Collins, both born in Cardiff, Wales, and both nurtured in the afterglow of the Welsh Revival, made their way there and took something of the revival with them.

Eventually their journey brought them to Houston, Texas, to be with family in their retirement years. There I would come to know them. They would become the face of Wales for me. Their countenances and, more important, their hearts show the afterglow of the spiritual awakening that once swept their country.

Mike was born in a low-income household near Cardiff's bustling docks. He went to work there and expected to spend a lifetime servicing the big ships sailing in from faraway places. He could not have anticipated on those grueling days that he would spend a good part of his life in faraway places.

Mike and his family were not religious in his early days, yet he says his earliest impressions of the world around him while he was growing up in south Wales "were of great respect for the Lord's Day, for close family and community relationships, and watching your language."

All of it, he thinks, was the afterglow of the revival.

Mike cannot remember any of his older relatives being Christians, yet as a youth, he heard them speak sometimes "of the religious and beneficial effects" remembered from the days when they were young. These kinfolk were all born in the immediate aftermath of the revival, and "were influenced by the commitment of believers, especially in the local Baptist church and the Salvation Army"— both of which had been impacted by the revival.

In fact, it was in the Baptist church that Mike came to know Christ. He was influenced by older Christians who were a generation removed from the era of the revival but still, he says, "under the influence and very dedicated to their ministry."

Mike was surprised—especially as a dockworker—when God called him into ministry, as were his church leaders. "It was unusual for a not-well-educated young person with no university degree to request a recommendation from the church to enter theological training for the ministry," he remembers these many years later.

Eventually Mike entered South Wales Baptist College, one of the departments of the School of Theology of the University of Wales. Mike knew God had called him to be a missionary, and he was determined to press on.

Before going to Brazil, the field of his calling, Mike served as pastor of a church in one of South Wales's valleys. He came to know older folk who still remembered the glory days of the revival during their youth. What he heard from them only intensified his grief at watching "very rapid" declines in all Welsh denominations. There was "a sad and disastrous loss of commitment and the consequent loss of vitality," he says. The effects of the revival might have been more enduring in Wales had there been in 1904–5 "a greater emphasis on solid biblical preaching."

"This is not to say there were not great Bible-believing preachers, but the major consequence seems to have been experiencing the power more than understanding the Word," Mike says. "This may have given entrance to the crippling liberal theology that gained preeminence in later years."

Nevertheless, Mike says he is "deeply thankful to God that I was saved through the ministry of a church led by godly pastors and lay leaders, who, in turn were influenced by those who had been touched in one way or another by the Revival."

Hazel was raised in a Christian family. Her parents were born in the revival era, in 1903 and 1906. She remembers her maternal grandfather talking about the revival. Hazel made her own commitment to Christ on March 13, 1951, in an evangelistic campaign in Cardiff led by Alan Redpath and Stephen Olford.

At age fifteen, Hazel began to sense God's call to missions. She moved to London to attend university and came under the influence of a man who knew the Welsh Revival up close from intense research. Hazel joined London's Westminster Chapel, where Martyn Lloyd Jones was pastor. Lloyd Jones had worked closely with Eifion Evans in researching and writing about the revival. Hazel says that this man who was so intimately acquainted with the Welsh Revival was "the most influential preacher and teacher" for her and others in their younger years.

One day in February 1970, Hazel was attending a ladies Bible study. The focus was John 15:16–17:

> You did not choose Me but I chose you, and appointed you that you would go and bear fruit, and that your fruit would remain, so that whatever you ask of the Father in My name He may give to you. This I command you, that you love one another.

In that moment, that *Logos* Word became *rhema*, God's utterance to Hazel. She knew for certain that God was calling her to be a missionary. In September 1971, Mike and Hazel arrived at a language school in Campinas, Saõ Paulo, Brazil.

Mike and Hazel spent their career in that great South American country, working in many capacities. Mike focused on evangelism and discipleship training and development and served as a seminary teacher, human needs coordinator, and chaplain at a maximum-security prison. He says now that this varied scope of work was an "extremely fulfilling experience."

Hazel worked in women's and children's ministries and wrote for a children's magazine in Brazil, a task which she ultimately was able to turn over to Brazilian women. She helped build a Sunday school ministry and served in street ministry and in the vast slums.

Revival, says Mike, "is a consequence of a number of concerns on the part of believers, but also a preparation for things to follow."

Though they are officially retired, Mike and Hazel make yearly trips back to Brazil to work alongside the people they led to Christ and discipled. They also serve in Houston, their newly adopted hometown.

Wherever they go, they and others like them are something of the afterglow of the lightning that struck their native land more than a century ago.

Acknowledgments

In addition to Mike and Hazel Collins, there are others to whom I am grateful for insight, inspiration, spiritual support, guidance, and encouragement.

My wife, Irene, is noted in our family and circle of friends as a woman of great wisdom. In fact, I often say she is the best theologian in our family. I am so grateful to God for allowing us fifty-six years of marriage (as I write these words) and pray He will bless us with more. *I* have no ministry, but *we* have a ministry, and I am thankful for her dedication and commitment.

Joel Kneedler is not only my publisher but also a dear friend whose walk with the Lord is an inspiration to me. He not only talks the talk but walks the walk.

I have had the privilege of working with Janene MacIvor on previous projects, and I respect her Christian spirit and highly professional editing abilities.

Joey Paul was my substantive editor on the book, and I borrow the meaning of Michelangelo's famous quote in thanking him for carving away at the hunk of an 84,000-word manuscript until its final 64,000-word form was set free.

ACKNOWLEDGMENTS

I thank Donald Mitchell, librarian at the Union School of Theology, Bridgend, Wales, for his extraordinary kindness in gathering and sending vital research materials used throughout this book.

In Houston, attorney Mark Lanier, himself an avid Bible student and teacher, has developed the Lanier Theological Library, a remarkable center for study and research. I thank Mark and his staff for their courtesies in allowing me to access important writings crucial to my research.

The staff at Fort Worth's Southwestern Baptist Theological Seminary, my beloved alma mater, must also be included in these acknowledgments. I appreciate their readiness to help as well as their expert assistance in accessing materials for this project.

Notes

Introduction

1. Blaise Pascal, *The Thoughts of Blaise Pascal*, ed. C. Kegan Paul, trans. from text of M. Auguste Molinier (London: George Bell and Sons, 1889).
2. Pascal, *Thoughts of Blaise Pascal*.

Chapter 1: We Need Lightning Now!

1. Lewis Drummond, *The Awakening That Must Come* (Nashville: Broadman, 1978), 18.
2. Brynmor Pierce Jones, *An Instrument of Revival: The Complete Life of Evan Roberts, 1878–1951* (South Plainfield, NJ: Bridge Publishing, 1995), 227.
3. Quoted in Jones, *Instrument of Revival*, 25.
4. Quoted in Jones, *Instrument of Revival*, 23.
5. Jones, *Instrument of Revival*, 23.
6. Quoted in Jones, *Instrument of Revival*, 24.
7. R. Tudur Jones, *Faith and the Crisis of a Nation: Wales 1890–1914*, ed. Robert Pope, trans. Sylvia Prys Jones (Cardiff: University of Wales Press, 2004), 311.
8. Roger Cohen, "The Great Unraveling," *New York Times*, September 15, 2014, http://www.nytimes.com/2014/09/16/opinion/roger-cohen-the-great-unraveling.html?_r=0.

9. Quoted in D. M. Phillips, *Evan Roberts: The Great Welsh Revivalist and His Work* (London: Marshall Brothers, 1923), http://www.welshrevival.org/biographies/phillips/001.htm.

10. David Matthews, *I Saw the Welsh Revival* (Chicago: Moody Press, 1951), https://www.gospeltruth.net/Isawthewelsh.htm.

11. H. Elvet Lewis, G. Campbell Morgan, and I. V. Neprash, *Glory Filled the Land: A Trilogy on the Welsh Revival of 1904–1905*, ed. Richard Owen Roberts (Wheaton, IL: International Awakening Press, 1989), 6.

12. Lewis, Morgan, and Neprash, *Glory Filled the Land*, 5.

13. Sources for Revival outcomes include: Malcolm McDow and Alvin L. Reid, *Firefall: How God Has Shaped History Through Revivals* (Nashville: Broadman & Holman Publishers, 1997); Jones, *Instrument of Revival*; Jones, *Faith and the Crisis of a Nation*; Eifion Evans, *The Welsh Revival of 1904* (Bridgend: Evangelical Press of Wales, 1969); Lewis, Morgan, and Neprash, *Glory Filled the Land*; and Matthews, *I Saw the Welsh Revival*.

14. Phillips, *Evan Roberts*.

15. J. Vynrwy Morgan, *The Welsh Religious Revival, 1904–5: A Retrospect and a Criticism* (Weston Rhyn: Quinta Press, 2004), http://www.welshrevival.org/histories/morgan/01.htm.

16. Quoted in Phillips, *Evan Roberts*, http://www.welshrevival.org/biographies/phillips/001.htm.

17. "Great Crowds of People Drawn to Loughor, Congregations Stay Until Half Past Two in the Morning," *Western Mail* (Cardiff, Wales), November 10, 1904. Quoted in Rick Joyner, *The World on Fire: The Welsh Revival and Its Lessons for Our Time* (Fort Mill, SC: MorningStar Publications, Inc., 2013), loc. 654 of 2149, Kindle.

18. Morgan, *Welsh Religious Revival*, 37, http://www.welshrevival.org/histories/morgan/01.htm.

19. George Campbell Morgan, quoted in McDow and Reid, *FireFall*, 279.

20. Quoted in Roland H. Bainton, *Here I Stand: A Life of Martin Luther* (Nashville: Abingdon, 1950), 49.

Chapter 2: The Times and Seasons of True Revival

1. Lewis, Morgan, and Neprash, *Glory Filled the Land*, 17ff.
2. Eifion Evans, *Revivals: Their Rise, Progress and Achievements* (London: Evangelical Library, 1960), 7.
3. Evans, *Revivals*, 8.
4. David R. J. Ollerton, *The Revival's Children: Early Welsh Pentecostalism in the Growth of Bethlehem Pentecost Church, Cefn Cribwr* (Cardiff, Wales: D. R. J. Ollerton, 2000), 1.
5. Ollerton, *Revival's Children*, 1.
6. Matthews, *I Saw the Welsh Revival*, 21.
7. Evans, *Welsh Revival of 1904*, 14.
8. Drummond, *Awakening That Must Come*, 98.
9. Matthews, *I Saw the Welsh Revival*, 21.

Chapter 3: The Revival Cycle

1. James Burns, *Revival Now: A Jesus Awakening* (Savage, MN: Broadstreet, 2018), 1.
2. Aleksandr Solzhenitsyn, "Godlessness: the First Step to the Gulag," (London, Templeton Prize Lecture, May 10, 1983).
3. Edward E. Ericson Jr., "Solzhenitsyn—Voice from the Gulag," *Eternity* (October 1985): 23.
4. Evans, *Revivals*, 27.
5. Charles Colson with Ellen Santilli Vaughn, *Against the Night*: Living in the New Dark Ages (Ann Arbor, MI: Servant Publications, 1989), 23–24.
6. Evans, *Revivals*, 5.
7. Evans, *Revivals*, 6.
8. Colson, *Against the Night*.
9. Eifion Evans, *Howell Harris, Evangelist, 1714–1773* (Cardiff: University of Wales Press, 1974).
10. Evans, *Howell Harris*.

Chapter 4: The Tao of Lightning

1. Quoted in Jones, *Instrument of Revival*, 25.

2. See, for example, James Hannam, *God's Philosophers: How the Medieval World Laid the Foundations of Modern Science* (London: Icon Books, 2010).

3. David Horn and Gordon Isaac, *Great Awakenings: Historical Perspectives for Today* (Peabody, MA: Hendrickson, 2016), 59.

4. See Barna Group, "Competing Worldviews Influence Today's Christians," *Barna: Research Releases in Culture and Media*, May 9, 2017, https://www.barna.com/research/competing-worldviews-influence -todays-christians/.

5. Horn and Isaac, *Great Awakenings*, 59.

Chapter 5: The Hovering Cloud

1. McDow and Reid, *Firefall*, 4–5.

2. "The Loughor Railway Accident," *Southland Times*, November 29, 1904, https://paperspast.natlib.govt.nz/newspapers/ST19041129.2.43.

3. Lewis, Morgan, and Neprash, *Glory Filled the Land*, 33.

4. Matthews, *I Saw the Welsh Revival*, 21.

5. Morgan, *Welsh Religious Revival*, 13.

6. Morgan, *Welsh Religious Revival*, 7.

Chapter 6: The Ground Below

1. Quoted in McDow and Reid, *Firefall*, 14.

2. Quoted in McDow and Reid, *Firefall*, 14.

3. See "How to Know If You're About to Be Struck by Lightning," Daily Mail, July 30, 2013, http://www.dailymail.co.uk/news /article-2381677/How-know-youre-struck-lightning-Picture -brothers-hair-end-minutes-before.html.

4. Al Sundermeir, "The Most Terrifying Part About Getting Struck by Lightning Is What Happens to You Afterwards," *Business Insider*, April 20, 2016, http://www.businessinsider.com/what-to-expect-when -you-survive-lightning-2016–4.

5. Romano Guardini, *The End of the Modern World: A Search for Orientation*, trans. Joseph Theman and Herbert Burke (New York: Sheed & Ward, 1956), 100–101.

6. James Strong, *Strong's Expanded Exhaustive Concordance of the Bible* (Nashville: Thomas Nelson, 2009), 2920, s.v. "krisis."

7. Evans, *Revivals*, 2–4.

8. Guardini, *End of the Modern World*, 100.

9. McDow and Reid, *Firefall*, 7.

10. Jones, *Instrument of Revival*, 151.

11. Matthew Arnold, "Dover Beach" (1867), https://www.poetryfoundation.org/poems/43588/dover-beach.

12. Christopher Dawson, *The Judgment of the Nations* (New York: Sheed and Ward, 1942), 98.

13. Dawson, *Judgment of the Nations*, 144.

14. David Edward PIke, "Dean Howell and the Welsh Revival," *Welldigger* (blog), January 14, 2015, http://daibach-welldigger.blogspot.com/2015/01/dean-howell-and-welsh-revival.html.

15. Evans, *Welsh Revival of 1904*, 41.

16. Jones, *Faith and the Crisis of a Nation*, 193.

17. Jones, *Faith and the Crisis of a Nation*,193.

18. W. E. Sangster, *Revival: The Need and the Way*, Westminster Pamphlet No. 7 (London: Epworth Press, 1957).

19. Sangster, *Revival*.

20. Evans, *Welsh Revival of 1904*.

Chapter 7: The Church and Revival

1. Material for this section comes from Tom DeLay and Wallace Henley, *Revival! Revolution! Rebirth!: A Radical Call from the Former Majority Leader of the United States House of Representatives* (Washington, DC: WND Books, 2016). I am also indebted to Eddie and Alice Smith, whose workshops and books on prayer have inspired people across the world, for awakening me to the concept of the church being like the House of Representatives.

2. Frances A. Schaeffer, *No Little People* (Wheaton, IL.: Crossway Books, 2003).

3. Quoted in McDow and Reid, *Firefall*, 54.

4. Evans, *Welsh Revival of 1904*, 49.

5. Quoted in William J. Murray, *Utopian Road to Hell: Enslaving America and the World with Central Planning* (Washington, DC: WND Books, 2016), 83.

Chapter 8: Evan Roberts and the Living Energy

1. Lewis A Drummond, *Spurgeon: Prince of Preachers* (Grand Rapids, MI: Kregel, 1992), 266.
2. Lewis, Morgan, and Neprash, *Glory Filled the Land*, xii–xiii.
3. Jones, *Instrument of Revival*, 95.
4. John Henry Newman, "The Pillar of the Cloud," June 16, 1833, http://www.newmanreader.org/works/verses/verse90.html.
5. Morgan, *Welsh Religious Revival*, http://www.welshrevival.org/histories/morgan/03.htm.
6. Jones, *Instrument of Revival*, 96.
7. Quoted in Jones, *Instrument of Revival*, 251.
8. Jones, *Faith and the Crisis of a Nation*, 37.
9. Jones, *Faith and the Crisis of a Nation*, 37.
10. Lewis, Morgan, and Neprash, *Glory Filled the Land*, 33.
11. Lewis, Morgan, and Neprash, *Glory Filled the Land*, 33.
12. Lewis, Morgan, and Neprash, *Glory Filled the Land*, 34.
13. Evans's parents had him baptized there not long after his birth in June 1878.
14. Matthews, *I Saw the Welsh Revival*, 25.
15. Jones, *Instrument of Revival*, 4.
16. Quoted in Lewis, Morgan, and Neprash, *Glory Filled the Land*, 34.
17. Lewis, Morgan, and Neprash, *Glory Filled the Land*, 35.
18. Phillips, *Evan Roberts*, loc. 770 of 6811, Kindle.
19. Quoted in Lewis, Morgan, and Neprash, *Glory Filled the Land*, 36.
20. Lewis, Morgan, and Neprash, *Glory Filled the Land*, 37.
21. Quoted in Lewis, Morgan, and Neprash, *Glory Filled the Land*, 37.
22. Quoted in Lewis, Morgan, and Neprash, *Glory Filled the Land*, 37.
23. Quoted in Lewis, Morgan, and Neprash, *Glory Filled the Land*, 38.
24. Quoted in Lewis, Morgan, and Neprash, *Glory Filled the Land*, 38.
25. John Hayward, "Timeline of the Background to 1904–5 Welsh

Revival," Version 2.3, July 2004, Church Growth Modelling, https://www.churchmodel.org.uk/Timelineback04.pdf.

26. Quoted in Phillips, *Evan Roberts*, loc. 2215 of 6811, Kindle.

27. Quoted in Phillips, *Evan Roberts*, loc, 2266 of 6811, Kindle.

Chapter 9: Many Rods

1. Robert Coleman, *Spark That Ignites: God's Promise to Revive the Church Through You* (Minneapolis: Worldwide Publications, 1989), 70.

2. Coleman, *Coming World Revival*, 83.

3. Emily Esfahani Smith, "You'll Never Be Famous—and That's O.K.," *New York Times*, September 4, 2017, https://www.nytimes.com /2017/09/04/opinion/middlemarch-college-fame.html.

4. Smith, "You'll Never Be Famous."

5. Keith Malcolmson, *Pentecostal Pioneers Remembered* (Maitland, FL: Xulon Press, 2008).

6. Rick Joyner, *The World Aflame: The Welsh Revival and Its Lessons for Our Time* (Springdale, PA: Whitaker House, 2012), loc. 390 of 2149, Kindle.

7. Joyner, *World Aflame*, loc. 390 of 2149, Kindle.

8. David Edward Pike, "The 1904-5 Revival in Clydach Vale, Rhondda," *Welldigger* (blog), October 24, 2013, http://daibach-welldigger. blogspot.com/2013/10/; and David Edward Pike, "Florrie Evans: The Girl Who Started a Revival," *Welldigger* (blog), October 11, 2015, http://daibach-welldigger.blogspot.com/2015/10/the-story-of-girl -who-began-revival.html.

9. Pike, "Florrie Evans."

10. Pike, "Florrie Evans."

11. Pike, "Florrie Evans."

12. Pike, "Florrie Evans."

13. Jones, *Faith and the Crisis of a Nation*, 286.

14. Pike, "Florrie Evans."

15. Evans, *Welsh Revival of 1904*, 54.

16. Jones, *Faith and the Crisis of a Nation*, 284.

17. Jones, *Faith and the Crisis of a Nation*, 285.

18. Jones, *Faith and the Crisis of a Nation*, 285.

19. Jones, *Faith and the Crisis of a Nation*, 285.

20. T. Mardy Rees, *Seth Joshua and Frank Joshua, the Renowned Evangelists: The Story of Their Wonderful Life-Work* (Wrexham: Hughes & Son, 1926), http://www.revival-library.org/index.php /catalogues-menu/1904/seth-and-frank-joshua.

21. Rees, *Seth Joshua and Frank Joshua*.

22. Rees, *Seth Joshua and Frank Joshua*.

23. Rees, *Seth Joshua and Frank Joshua*, part II, chapter 2, http://www .revival-library.org/index.php/catalogues-menu/1904/seth-and -frank-joshua.

24. Matthews, *I Saw the Welsh Revival*, 28–29.

25. Jones, *Faith and the Crisis of a Nation*, 290.

26. Matthews, *I Saw the Welsh Revival*, 27–28.

Chapter 10: Dynamics of the Lightning

1. Richard Owen Roberts, *Revival!* (Wheaton, IL: Tyndale House, 1982), 16–17.

2. Jones, *Instrument of Revival*, 166–67.

3. Schaeffer, *No Little People*, 66.

4. McDow and Reid, *Firefall*, 7.

5. Lewis, Morgan, and Neprash, *Glory Filled the Land*, 5.

6. Lewis, Morgan, and Neprash, *Glory Filled the Land*, 9.

7. Jones, *Faith and the Crisis of a Nation*, 107.

8. Jones, *Faith and the Crisis of a Nation*, 110.

9. Jones, *Faith and the Crisis of a Nation*, 110.

10. Lewis, Morgan, and Neprash, *Glory Filled the Land*, 15.

11. Quoted in Lewis, Morgan, and Neprash, *Glory Filled the Land*, 15.

12. Ilsley W. Charlton, *The Revival in Wales: Some Facts and Some Lessons* (London: Jarrold & Sons, 1905), 9ff.

13. Evans, *Welsh Revival of 1904*, 10–11.

14. Matthews, *I Saw the Welsh Revival*, 77–78.

Chapter 11: Handling the Lightning

1. Quoted in Charles E. Hummel, *Fire in the Fireplace: Contemporary Charismatic Renewal* (Downers Grove, IL: InterVarsity Press, 1978), 15.
2. "Theology: The God Is Dead Movement," *Time*, October 22, 1965, http://content.time.com/time/subscriber/article/0,33009,941410,00.html.
3. John Newport, *The New Age Movement and the Biblical Worldview* (Grand Rapids: Eerdmans, 1998), 512.
4. Newport, *New Age Movement*, 512.
5. "Sacred Places of Sedona, Arizona," Inner Journey, http://www.sedona-spiritualretreats.com/sacred-places.html.
6. Lewis, Morgan, and Neprash, *Glory Filled the Land*, 92.
7. Quoted in Evans, *Welsh Revival of 1904*, 195.
8. Evans, *Welsh Revival of 1904*, 195–96.
9. Evans, *Welsh Revival of 1904*, 163.
10. David F. Wells, *No Place for Truth: Or Whatever Happened to Evangelical Theology?* (Grand Rapids: Eerdmans, 1993), 267–68.
11. Wells, *No Place for Truth*, 104.
12. Evans, *Welsh Revival of 1904*, 6.
13. F. B. Meyer, a noted Christian leader of the time, was so concerned about Morgan's book that Meyer wrote him saying he hoped "nothing of adverse criticism of the past may affect either him [Evan Roberts] or the work of God through him." Cited in Evans, *Welsh Revival of 1904*, 173.
14. Morgan, *Welsh Religious Revival*, 50–51.
15. Quoted in Evans, *Welsh Revival of 1904*, 5.
16. Strong, *Strong's Expanded Exhaustive Concordance*, 5010, s.v. "taxis."
17. Evans, *Welsh Revival of 1904*, 6.

Chapter 12: Revival and Spiritual Warfare

1. See Roger Luckhurst, "WT Snead, a Forgotten Victim of Titanic," *The Telegraph*, April 10, 2012, http://www.telegraph.co.uk/history/titanic-anniversary/9195793/WT-Stead-a-forgotten-victim-of-Titanic.html.

2. W. T. Stead, *If Christ Came to Chicago: A Plea for the Union of All Who Love in the Service of All Who Suffer* (Chicago: Laird & Lee, 1894).

3. Evan Roberts, Arthur Goodrich, G. Campbell Morgan, W. T. Stead, Evan Henry Hopkins, and E. W. Moore, *The Story of the Welsh Revival as Told by Eyewitnesses: Together with a Sketch of Evan Roberts and His Message to the World* (New York: Fleming H. Revell, 1905); Stead's account is available online at https://attackingthedevil.co.uk /steadworks/roberts.php.

4. Matthews, *I Saw the Welsh Revival*, 22.

5. Sangster, *Revival*.

6. All quotations from Sangster in this chapter [or section] are from Sangster, *Revival*, quoted in Robert Evans, "An Evangelical World-View Philosophy," Research in Evangelical Revivals (website), PDF, https:// revivalsresearch.net/docs/EvangelicalWorldViewPhilosophy.pdf.

7. Matthews, *I Saw the Welsh Revival*, 69.

8. Lewis, Morgan, and Neprash, *Glory Filled the Land*, 158.

9. Matthews, *I Saw the Welsh Revival*, 70.

10. Charlton, *The Revival in Wales*, 24.

11. Charlton, *The Revival in Wales*, 25.

12. Lewis, Morgan, and Neprash, *Glory Filled the Land*, 80.

13. Matthews, *I Saw the Welsh Revival*, 125.

14. Evans, *Welsh Revival of 1904*, 125.

15. Peter and Dorothy Bennett, *The Quarry Revival* (Llanfairfechan, Wales: Turning Point, 1992), 37.

16. Evans, *Welsh Revival of 1904*, 126.

17. Evans, *Welsh Revival of 1904*, 125.

18. Sangster, *Revival*, 7.

19. Evans, *Welsh Revival of 1904*, 114–15.

20. Sangster, *Revival*, 8.

21. Sangster, *Revival*, 9.

22. Evans, *Welsh Revival of 1904*, 161.

23. Quoted in Emyr Roberts, *Revival and Its Fruit* (Brynitirion, Wales: Evangelical Library of Wales, 1981), 9.

24. Quoted in Roberts, *Revival and Its Fruit*, 9–10.

Chapter 13: The Weight of God's Glory

1. Roberts Liardon, *God's Generals: Evan Roberts* (New Kensington, PA: Whitaker House, 2012), loc. 450 of 470, Kindle.
2. Jones, *Instrument of Revival*, 28.
3. Jones, *Instrument of Revival*, 28
4. As cited in Evans, *Welsh Revival of 1904*, 173
5. E. Morgan Humphreys, *Gwyr Enwog Gynt, II* (Aberystwyth, 1953), 100–109, as quoted in Jones, *Faith and the Crisis of a Nation*, 361–62.
6. Drummond, *Awakening That Must Come*, 102.
7. Jessie Penn-Lewis with Evan Roberts, *War on the Saints* (1912, reprint; Springdale, PA: Whitaker House, 1996).
8. Jones, *Instrument of Revival*, 102.
9. "News from Wales," *Scranton Truth*, May 13, 1905, cited in Edwin J. Orr, *The Flaming Tongue: The Impact of Twentieth Century Revivals* (Chicago: Moody Press, 1973), which is cited online at Robert Pear, "Evan Roberts," Revival Resource Center, January 16, 2017, http://godsgeneralsandrevivals.com/?p=1172.
10. Lewis, Morgan, and Neprash, *Glory Filled the Land*, 94.
11. Quoted in Jones, *Instrument of Revival*, 95.
12. Danica Kirka, "Britain's Queen Dishes on Weight of the Crown in Documentary," *U.S. News and World Report*, January 12, 2018, https://www.usnews.com/news/world/articles/2018-01-12/monarch-discusses-weight-of-the-crown-in-documentary.
13. Quoted in Jones, *Instrument of Revival*, 97.
14. Evans, *Welsh Revival of 1904*, 66.
15. Evans, *Welsh Revival of 1904*, 78.
16. Evans, *Welsh Revival of 1904*, 78.
17. Evans, *Welsh Revival of 1904*, 80.
18. Matthews, *I Saw the Welsh Revival*, 123–24.

Chapter 14: The Reach of the Revival

1. Roberts et al., *The Story of the Welsh Revival*, 6, quoted in McDow and Reid, *Firefall*, 275.
2. McDow and Reid, *Firefall*, 295.

3. Jin-Heon Jung, "Underground Railroads of Christian Conversion: North Korean Migrants and Evangelical Missionary Networks in Northeast Asia," *Cultural Diversity in China* 1, no. 2 (2015): 179.

4. David Edward Pike, "The Welsh Revival and Europe (1) Scandinavia," *Welldigger*, September 17, 2017, https://daibach-welldigger.blogspot.com/2017/09/the-welsh-revival-and-europe-1.html?view=magazine.

5. Lewis, Morgan, and Neprash, *Glory Filled the Land*, 59

6. Lewis, Morgan, and Neprash, *Glory Filled the Land*, 63.

7. Frank Bartleman, *Azusa Street* (1925, reprint; Plainfield, NJ: Logos International, 1980), 7.

8. S. B. Shaw, *The Great Revival in Wales* (Chicago: Shaw, 1905).

9. George T. B. Davis, "Thirty-Four Thousand Conversions in Wales," *New York Weekly Witness*, quoted in Shaw, *Great Revival in Wales*, 50, http://www.welshrevival.org/histories/shaw/07.htm; Horn and Isaac, *Great Awakenings*, 68–69.

10. Davis, "Thirty-Four Thousand Conversions in Wales."

11. Horn and Isaac, *Great Awakenings*, 69.

12. Horn and Isaac, *Great Awakenings*, 70.

13. Horn and Isaac, *Great Awakenings*, 70.

14. Horn and Isaac, *Great Awakenings*, 71.

15. Vinson Synan, "Pentecostalism: William Seymour," *Christian History*, no. 65 (2000), http://www.christianitytoday.com/history/issues/issue-65/pentecostalism-william-seymour.html.

16. For more of the history of William Seymour, Frank Bartleman, and Azusa Street, see "Azusa Street Testimonies," 312 Azusa Street, http://www.azusastreet.org/AzusaStreetBartleman.htm.

17. Wes Granberg-Michaelson, "Think Christianity Is Dying? No, Christianity Is Shifting Dramatically," *Washington Post*, May 20, 2015, https://www.washingtonpost.com/news/acts-of-faith/wp/2015/05/20/think-christianity-is-dying-no-christianity-is-shifting-dramatically/?utm_term=.6f4a30b6d129.

18. Philip Jenkins, *The Next Christendom: The Coming of Global Christianity* (New York: Oxford University Press, 2011), 1.

19. Mathias D. Thelen, "The Explosive Growth of Pentecostal-Charismatic Christianity in the Global South, and Its Implications for Catholic Evangelization," Homiletic and Pastoral Review, June 28, 2017, http://www.hprweb.com/2017/06/the-explosive-growth-of-pentecostal-charismatic-christianity-in-the-global-south-and-its-implications-for-catholic-evangelization/.

20. Ralph Martin, The Catholic Church at the End of an Age: What Is the Spirit Saying? (San Francisco: Ignatius, 1994), 87, quoted in Thelen, "Explosive Growth of Pentecostal-Charismatic Christianity."

21. Evans, Welsh Revival of 1904, has provided much information in this chapter and I follow Evans's sequence here.

22. Jones, Instrument of Revival, 68.

23. Jones, Instrument of Revival, 76.

24. Lewis, Morgan, and Neprash, Glory Filled the Land, 181.

25. Lewis, Morgan, and Neprash, Glory Filled the Land, 200.

26. Evans, Welsh Revival of 1904, 120.

27. Evans, Welsh Revival of 1904, 120.

28. Evans, Welsh Revival of 1904, 149.

29. Evans, Welsh Revival of 1904, 150.

30. Evans, Welsh Revival of 1904, 151.

31. Evans, Welsh Revival of 1904, 152.

32. Evans, Welsh Revival of 1904, 153.

33. Evans, Welsh Revival of 1904, 154.

34. Quoted in S. G. Pothan, The Syrian Christians of Kerala (New York: Asia Publishing House, 1963), 25.

35. Larry V. Brown, "The Welsh Revival and Other Revivals Worldwide, 1900–1910," May 9, 2013, http://www.academia.edu/3881886/THE_WELSH_REVIVAL_AND_OTHER_REVIVALS_WORLDWIDE_1900–1910.

Chapter 15: Why Revival Tapers

1. Leonard Ravenhill, Why Revival Tarries (Minneapolis: Bethany House, 1959).

2. Robert Coleman, "The Spark That Ignites," Cru.Comm, February 24, 2018, https://www.cru.org/content/dam/cru/legacy/2012/04/colemanthesparkthatignites.pdf.

3. Jones, *Faith and the Crisis of a Nation*, 329.

4. Findley B. Edge, *A Quest for Vitality in Religion: A Theological Approach to Religious Education*, rev. ed. (Macon, GA: Smyth & Helwys, 1994), 19.

5. Edge, *Quest for Vitality in Religion*, 20.

6. McDow and Reid, *Firefall*, 139.

7. McDow and Reid, *Firefall*, 139.

8. McDow and Reid, *Firefall*, 139.

9. McDow and Reid, *Firefall*, 143.

10. Joyner, *World on Fire*, loc. 1421 of 2149, Kindle.

11. Joyner, *World on Fire*, loc. 1461 of 2149, Kindle.

12. Liardon, *God's Generals*, loc. 291 of 470, Kindle.

13. Liardon, *God's Generals*, loc. 328 of 470, Kindle.

14. Liardon, *God's Generals*, loc. 320 of 470, Kindle.

15. Liardon, *God's Generals*, loc. 359 of 470, Kindle.

16. Jones, *Faith and the Crisis of a Nation*, 173.

17. Jones, *Faith and the Crisis of a Nation*, 173.

18. Jones, *Faith and the Crisis of a Nation*, 165.

19. Jones, *Faith and the Crisis of a Nation*, 165.

Chapter 16: Jubilee

1. Robert Coleman, *The Coming World Revival: Your Part in God's Plan to Reach the World* (Wheaton: Crossway Books, 1995), 159. Coleman is the director of the School of World Mission and Evangelism and a professor of evangelism at Trinity Evangelical Divinity School.

2. Tom Phillips, *Jesus Now: God Is Up to Something Big* (Racine, WI: Broadstreet, 2016). Phillips is vice president of the Billy Graham Evangelistic Association.

3. Edwin B. May, "Extensive Oxygen Depletion in Mobile Bay, Alabama," *Limnology and Oceanography* 18, no. 3 (1973): 353–66.

4. Billy Graham, "The King Is Coming," *Let the Earth Hear His Voice*,

Official Reference Volume for the International Congress on World Evangelization, Lausanne, Switzerland, ed. J. Douglas (Minneapolis: World Wide Publications, 1975), 1466.

5. McDow and Reid, *Firefall*, 334.

6. Lewis, Morgan, and Neprash, *Glory Filled the Land*, 83.

7. W. T. Stead, *The Revival in the West*, 3rd ed. (London: Review of Reviews, 1905), 36–37, http://www.welshrevival.org/histories/stead1/02.htm.

8. Lewis, Morgan, and Neprash, *Glory Filled the Land*, 60.

9. Phillips, *Jesus Now*, 154.

10. Coleman, *Coming World Revival*, 151.

11. Coleman, *Coming World Revival*, 157.

12. Coleman, *Coming World Revival*, 163.

13. Coleman, *Coming World Revival*, 150.

About the Author

Wallace Henley is senior associate pastor at Houston's Second Baptist Church. He is a professional journalist and former White House and congressional aide. Wallace is the architect of Belhaven University's Master of Ministry Leadership degree. He is author of more than twenty books, including *God and Churchill*, written with Jonathan Sandys, great-grandson of Sir Winston Churchill. Wallace has also collaborated on books by Ed Young, pastor of Second Baptist Church, Houston.

Wallace and Irene were married in 1961 and have two children, six grandchildren, and four great-grandchildren.

Wallace was born December 5, 1941, in Birmingham, Alabama. He studied at Samford University, Southwestern Baptist Theological Seminary, and Trinity Theological Seminary, and holds a master's degree in ministry (with high distinction), with a focus on leadership.

Wallace began his career as a reporter, columnist, and editor at Alabama's *Birmingham News*. He won several journalism awards, including an Associated Press award for his coverage of Birmingham's civil rights movement. In 1970, President Richard Nixon appointed

Wallace as assistant director of the Cabinet Committee on Education, and Wallace served at the White House until 1973.

Not long after leaving Washington, Wallace sensed the renewal of a call to church ministry he had first experienced at fifteen. He became the pastor of churches in Alabama and Texas.

Because of his experience at the White House and global travels with Dr. John Edmund Haggai, founder of Haggai Institute, since 1969 Wallace has had a strong interest in world affairs and equipping biblically trained leadership. Upon the collapse of communism he conducted leadership conferences in several former Soviet states. He has spoken extensively at conferences in Asia, Africa, Europe, and Latin America, as well as in the United States.

Wallace is a child of revival, having given his life to Christ during a revival meeting in 1956. He is passionate in his belief that only true revival can rescue the nations in our age of crisis. He brings that passion into the pages of *Call Down Lightning*.